Among Friends
~ More Scrap Quilts

by
Brenda Henning

Bear Paw Productions
4015 Iona Circle
Anchorage, AK 99507

Dedication

This book is dedicated to my children, Beth, Christi and Joshua. Without my girls, I would not have been able to keep up the busy pace this spring. Josh makes life interesting at all times.

Acknowledgements

Many thanks to the girls who shared their quilts with us: Debbie Repasky, Diana Bradley, and Pam Ventgen.

Credits

Written and illustrated by Brenda Henning.
Edited by Marcia Harmening.
Photography by Randy Brandon,
    Third Eye Photography.
Machine quilting by Norma Kindred.
Printed in the United States of America.

ISBN 0-9648878-4-3

Among Friends - More Scrap Quilts©
© 1998 by Brenda Henning
Bear Paw Productions
4015 Iona Circle
Anchorage, AK 99507
(907)349-7873

Introduction

This book is a testimony to my continued love of scrap quilts. My motto is - "Why use five fabrics when fifty will do the job?"

Fabric is such a soothing element in my life. I am able to satisfy the creative juices that flow while producing an article that is useful for my everyday life.

Quilts can be used for beds, wall hangings, and couch throws. Quilts can be a comfort to those who are ill, warmth for those who are cold, and safety for the child in all of us. Quilts can be the holder of memories when made with fabrics that bring us back to a time long forgotten.

The patterns contained in these pages are great when constructed by the many friends in your quilting circle. The scrappy nature of the designs lend themselves well to the variety of fabrics that can be found in the collections of your nearest and dearest quilting friends. Besides, what is a little fabric between friends?

This book has been written and edited while on the road. The trip has been titled the five week trip to insanity. Portions where written while at a conference in Bend, Oregon; on a Pacific beach in southern Oregon; at my in-laws house in Minnesota; and on a ferry boat cruising up the Alaska Inside Passage. Why is this the trip to "insanity"? Because the trip is being made with our three children in a pop-up camper. There is definitely "no place like home!"

Contents

General Directions

I hope that you will take the time to read through this first chapter before cutting fabrics for your favorite scrap quilt. You will find that many of the questions you might have about my approach to piecing will be answered in the following pages.

The yardages listed for each quilt pattern have been rounded up slightly to allow for the fact that "scrap" quilts tend to use more fabric than one would normally use. Multiple strips are used incompletely at times to create the greatest diversity in the fabric selection.

Yardage has been based upon 42" wide fabric. If your fabric is substantially wider or narrower after prewashing, your yardage requirement may also need adjustment.

1/4" seams are used throughout the piecing. The cutting instructions given for each piece refer to the actual cut size. The 1/4" seam allowance has been added to all dimensions. Check the accuracy of your seams before you begin. You will find a simple "1/4" seam test" in the following pages. Accuracy is important to the success of your quilt. In the case of a quilt with a pieced border, the piecing of the body of the quilt will determine if the border fits properly! The measurements given are all mathematically correct; it is assumed that your piecing will also be correct.

Cutting instructions assume that all strips are cut the width of the fabric, measured selvage to selvage. This strip should measure 42" or longer. Do not cut the strip to this length.

Half square triangle units are made from layered fabric squares or rectangles using **triangle foundation papers**. The triangle foundation paper method allows for accurate results. Master foundation papers have been provided on pages 86

and 87. You may trace or photocopy the number of foundations that you need. Triangle foundation papers are available preprinted. Check with your local quilt shop for availability. Standard cutting instructions have been included for those who choose to use traditional methods.

Specialty rulers are used to construct some patterns. Wherever appropriate, a brand name has been mentioned. Ask your local quilt shop if these rulers are available, or contact the manufacturer directly to purchase the ruler indicated. A template will also be given in these situations. I am a gadget person; if a ruler exists that will make my quilting easier, I will surely buy it!

Refer to the "Finishing" chapter for border questions. The quilts in this book were constructed using square borders. The **final border** on all quilts has been cut on the lengthwise grain of the fabric. The final border yardage reflects the lengthwise grain cut.

Fabric Preparation

Fabric preparation should be handled in the same manner that the completed quilt will be cared for. I recommend prewashing all fabrics. As each piece enters my house, the first stop is the laundry room. All fabric in my personal stash has been washed using Orvus paste (a horse shampoo) or Dreft. Do not use detergent to wash your fabrics because detergents act to strip color from cotton fabrics.

To replace the firmness of the sizing that has been washed out of the fabric, press all fabrics using a heavy spray starch or spray sizing. The fabric that is prepared in this way will behave much better when pressing seams. Bias edges will be more stable and less likely to stretch. You will find that piecing is much easier with fabric that doesn't stretch out of shape so quickly.

Rotary Cutting Tools

The rotary cutter is a razor knife that resembles a pizza cutter. The blade is very sharp and deserves to be treated with utmost respect. This amazing tool has revolutionized quilt making, nearly replacing scissors. I recommend a rotary cutter that has a manual safety guard. Some rotary cutters available on the market have a spring-loaded guard that can accidentally retract when dropped, exposing the razor sharp blade and cutting your hand or foot. The spring-loaded guards protect you from only the most minor of blade "bumps." The rotary cutters that have a manually closing safety guard, such as Olfa® and Fiskar®, require that you consciously close the guard after every cut. Learn to make a habit of closing the guard every time!! An exposed blade on the work surface can lead to tragic results, accidentally cut fabric or worse — cut fingers and bloodstained fabric. Do not leave a rotary cutter unattended around a curious toddler or young child.

I prefer to use the Olfa® rotary cutter. This particular rotary cutter can be used both right and left-handed without repositioning the blade.

To ensure the life of the blade, the rotary cutter must be used only on a compatible cutting surface. The self-healing cutting mats are a necessary tool. While the mats come in many sizes, purchase the largest cutting mat that you can afford. The 24" x 36" cutting mat is worth every dime.

Omnigrid® is my ruler of preference. The Omnigrid® brand is the most accurate of all rulers that I have worked with. It is very important that all of your rulers are accurate and agree with each other. Compare the markings of all rulers in your collection. If any ruler does not measure up, discard it!! The markings on your rotary mat must also agree with the rulers you have chosen to use.

Squaring Up Yardage

•Fold your fabric in half lengthwise, wrong sides together, selvage edges even. You may need to shift one selvage to the right or left to eliminate wrinkles along the folded edge. Once this has been accomplished, fold the fabric again, lengthwise, bringing the folded edge even with the selvage edges. The fabric will now be folded into four thicknesses, and measure about 10 1/2" wide, allowing strips to be cut without repositioning your ruler hand.

•Lay the folded fabric horizontally on your gridded cutting mat. The folded edge should be nearest you. Place the fold along a horizontal line of the mat. This will allow you to place your ruler along a vertical mat marking, guaranteeing a straight cut. If you are right-handed, the bulk of your fabric should be on the right, and you will start cutting from the left side. This will be reversed for a left-handed person.

•The rotary cutter is held with the blade perpendicular to the mat and against the edge of the ruler. The rotary cutter is held in the palm of your hand with the index finger on the ridged surface of the handle. This placement helps you to better control the rotary cutter. You are in effect pointing it in the proper direction.

•Cut away from yourself using one smooth even stroke. Do not make short choppy cuts which will create a ragged edge. The first cut will trim off the raw edge and square up the fabric. The clean edge will be perpendicular to the selvage. Trim sparingly to give the fabric a clean edge while wasting as little fabric as possible.

Cutting Strips

After the original cut has been made to square up the end of the yardage, you are ready to cut your first strip.

•Move the ruler to the right (left for a left-handed person) and align the squared off edge with the ruler marking for the strip width desired. Make sure that the correct marking lines up all along the cut edge, not just at one point!! Measure twice and cut once!!

•Cut along the right (left) side of the ruler. Be sure to keep your blade flush against the ruler; do not allow the ruler to shift. It may be helpful to hold the ruler with a finger or two off the left edge (right edge for a left-handed person). This will stabilize the ruler to prevent ruler slips. Lift the ruler and remove the strip without disturbing the yardage.

•Open the strip and look at it closely. The strip should be straight and of a consistent width. If your strip is not straight, refold your fabric and make certain that the edges are even. Also, make sure the original cut was made correctly, perpendicular to the folded edge.

•If it is necessary to cut a strip wider than your ruler, use the rulings of the cutting mat to measure the strip or square. Double check the mat measurements against those of your ruler to determine if the mat measurements are accurate.

Subcutting Strips

•Squares and rectangles needed for piecing will be cut from strips. Cut the strip to the required width

and open the double fold. You will be working with two layers of fabric and a single fold. If you are right handed, the selvages should be placed at the left. Trim off the first 1/2" to remove the selvages (more if needed) and square up the end of the strip. Use the mat markings to establish a perpendicular cut.

•Align the top edge of the ruler with the edge of the fabric, the bottom edge of the fabric should line up with a ruler marking. Cut the squares or rectangles to the required dimension. Continue cutting from the strip to satisfy the number needed.

•Diamonds are also cut from strips. The Scrap Hunter diamond is cut from a strip 2 3/8" wide.

•Diamonds are best cut from an open strip - only one layer is cut - or multiple layers are cut, with all layers facing right side up. This will place a straight of grain edge next to a bias edge when pieced, allowing for greater stability.

•Place the strip of fabric horizontally on the cutting mat. The 45° angle marking of the ruler will be positioned along the bottom edge of the strip. Trim the fabric extending from the left edge of the ruler -

turn the mat if necessary, to make the cut a right-handed cut. This establishes the true bias edge.

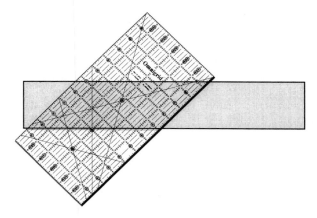

•Measure to the right of the newly cut bias edge using the rulings on your rotary ruler. Cut along the right edge of the ruler. The resulting diamond is a true 45° diamond. The sides are all the same length and the narrow angles measure 45°. Scrap Hunter diamonds are cut from a 2 3/8" wide strip. The secondary cut will measure 2 3/8" from the bias edge.

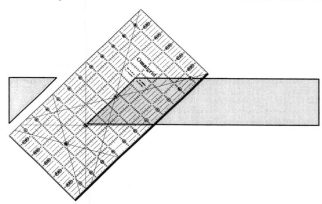

•Continue cutting diamonds from the strip. After cutting three or four diamonds, use the 45° angle marking of the rotary ruler to double check the bias angle of the strip. You may need to trim the bias edge to correct the angle.

Half Square Triangles

Half square triangles are literally triangles that are one half of a square. The square is cut once from corner to corner, diagonally. This places the grain of the fabric along the two short sides of the right triangle.

A half square triangle is one of the most basic shapes used in quiltmaking. Therefore, it is very important to know when to use this type of triangle. Half square triangles are used whenever the short side of the triangle will fall at the edge of a quilt block or quilt top. This allows for the greatest stability and the least amount of stretch in these much handled positions.

When working with templates, watch for the arrows that indicate grain (thread) lines. The location of these arrows will determine if the triangle is a half square triangle or a quarter square triangle (discussion to follow).

The formula below is very important for you to remember. It is the key to working with half square triangles!!

• Finished Size + 7/8″ = Cut Square •

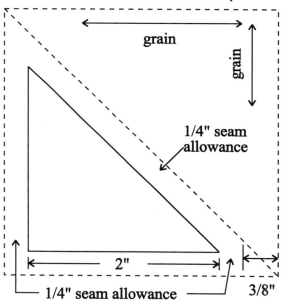

In the above diagram, 2" is the finished size of the triangle. As you can see, there is an additional 3/8" at the right that needs to be accounted for. Where does this 3/8" extension go when triangles are sewn together? These pieces are called "dog ears" and are trimmed from the completed unit. This eliminates bulk and prevents the shadow that a dog ear can create behind a light background fabric.

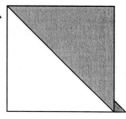

trimmed "dog ear"

Quarter Square Triangles

Quarter square triangles are one quarter of a square. The square is cut twice from corner to corner - diagonally. This places the grain of the fabric along the long side of the right triangle. The 3/8" extension occurs on both ends of the long side in the case of a quarter square triangle.

The formula for quarter square triangles is as follows:

•Finished Size + 1 1/4″ = Cut Square•

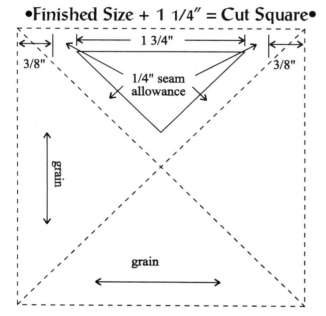

In the above diagram, 1 3/4″ is the finished size of the triangle. 1 3/4″ + 1 1/4″ = 3″ The square is cut 3″.

Quarter square triangles are not as common as their half square counterparts, but it is just as important to memorize the formula to avoid any possible mistakes that would place the bias along the edge of a block or quilt top.

Template Preparation and Use

Templates are necessary in the case of shapes that cannot be cut with a rotary cutter and standard rotary ruler. The pieces may be curved or involve angles that are not 30°, 60° or 45° angles.

Templates are generally made from frosted sheets of plastic that can be purchased at your local quilt shop. Template plastic is available with or without a 1/4″ grid. The plastic can be easily cut with paper scissors or a rotary cutter.

•Trace the template onto the plastic with a sharp pencil; I prefer to use a 0.5 mm mechanical lead pencil, it never dulls. It is helpful to use a small ruler to trace the straight lines.

•You may find that taping the plastic in place with drafting tape while tracing the template is necessary. Drafting tape removes easily from paper and will not harm your original pattern or book.

•Mark the grain line, if indicated, and all extra dots and lines that may be helpful as you construct the quilt block. It is a good idea to note block details on the template: such as the block name, block size, and template number or letter, if so titled.

•Very carefully, cut on the drawn line. Once the template is cut, place it on top of the original to make certain that the template has not "grown". It is very important that the template does not change size, shape, or angle.

Cut Once Diagonally

Fabric pieces that will be used as individual half square triangles will be cut as squares with the instructions to cut each square once diagonally as diagramed below. Cutting a square once diagonally places the stretchy bias edge along the long side of the triangle.

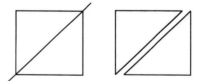

Cut Twice Diagonally

Fabric pieces that will be used as individual quarter square triangles will be cut as squares with the instructions to cut each square twice diagonally as diagramed below. Cutting a square twice diagonally places the stretchy bias edge along the two short sides of the triangle.

Machine Piecing

1/4" Seam Allowance

All of our seams will be sewn with a 1/4" seam allowance. It is of utmost importance to establish and maintain an accurate 1/4" seam allowance. Some of you already have quilting experience and feel confident that you know where your 1/4" seam is. I would encourage you to do the following exercise anyway. I find that many of my students have misjudged their seam allowance and have been able to correct it with this exercise.

You will actually be sewing with a **scant** 1/4" seam allowance. The difference will be taken up in the slight fold or "ridge" at the seam.

•To find your 1/4" seam allowance place a small ruler underneath your presser foot. When the needle is gently lowered, it should rest just to the right of the 1/4" mark on the right side of your ruler. If the needle were to pierce the ruler, the hole left by the needle would just graze the 1/4" marking on your ruler.

•With the presser foot holding the ruler in this position, carefully adjust the ruler so the markings on the left side of the ruler run parallel with the markings on the throat plate of your sewing machine.

•Once you are satisfied the ruler is positioned correctly, place a 1/2" x 3" strip of moleskin along the right edge of the ruler on the throat plate. Moleskin is a Dr. Scholl's® product, available at most groceries and pharmacies. The adhesive back of the moleskin will stick to the throat plate and give an edge to hold your seam allowance against. Moleskin gives more of an edge to follow than masking tape. It is not high enough that it will impede or pull out your pins.

1/4" Seam Test

•Cut 3 pieces of fabric 1 1/2" x 6". Sew these strips together along the lengthwise edge. Press the seams in one direction. After pressing, check that there are no "accordion" pleats at the seams. Press again if necessary.

•Measure your sewn unit, it should measure exactly 3 1/2" from raw edge to raw edge. The strips on either side should measure 1 1/4", and the center strip should measure 1" wide.

•If your sewn unit doesn't measure exactly 3 1/2", you will need to adjust your moleskin. If the sewn unit is **wider** than 3 1/2", your seam allowance is too narrow and the moleskin should be moved to the right. If the sewn strip is **narrower** than 3 1/2", your seam allowance is too wide and the moleskin should be moved to the left.

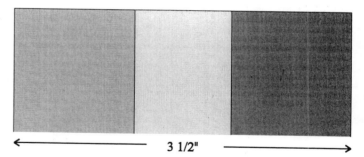

← —————————— 3 1/2" —————————— →

The amount that you need to move the moleskin is only one fourth of the amount that your strip differs from 3 1/2". Two seams are involved in the sewn strip, each seam involves two pieces of fabric —move the moleskin 1/4 of the difference.

It is a commonly held thought that the 1/4" seam allowance should be measured to check the accuracy of the stitching. Unfortunately, this does not work. The seam allowance is a scant 1/4". Measure the **finished dimension** of the fabric from the right side of the unit or quilt block.

I do not trust the 1/4" marking on my sewing machines. Usually the factory markings are accurate enough for clothing construction, but not for the precision demanded by quilting. I also do not recommend using the edge of your presser foot as a guide. Very few actually measure 1/4" from the needle.

If you have placed the moleskin exactly as described, and are still having problems stitching a 1/4" seam allowance, it may be your sewing machine that is being naughty. The feed dogs of some machines pull to the right, some to the left. Sewing machines are an eccentric lot! Adjust the moleskin to where the sewing machine demands that the edge of the fabric be held. This may not be at the mark 1/4" from the needle. Get to know your machine and work with its character flaws.

Strip Piecing

Not all piecing is accomplished by sewing individual squares and triangles together. Many units can be first sewn together in strip form and then, after the strips are subcut, the resulting units will be stitched together to form the intended square.

•The first step is to arrange the strips in the sequence that they will appear.

•Begin by sewing strips together in pairs.

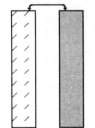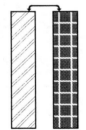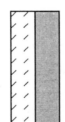

•After each pair is sewn, press the strips flat from the wrong side. This smoothes any wrinkles caused by poor thread tension and sets the seam. This is called setting the seam.

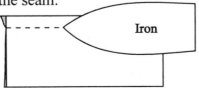

•Once you have set the seam, open the fabrics and press the seam from the right side. Pressing on the right side gives the visibility required to prevent accordion pleating at the seam. The seam allowances should be pressed in one direction for the greatest strength.

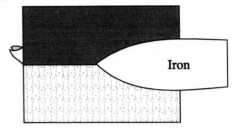

•Stitch strip pairs together and press.

•Once sewn and pressed, the strips may be subcut into the units necessary to complete the piecing of the block. Place the strip right side up on the cutting mat. Align a perpendicular marking of the ruler with a seam line and cut the strip to the width called for in the pattern.

•Reassemble the subcut units into the formation dictated by the pattern, stitch and press.

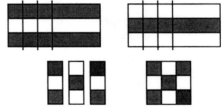

Chain Piecing

Chain piecing refers to the practice of stitching units one right after another without clipping the threads between the units. The first unit is stitched and left attached to the threads after passing under the presser foot. The second and following units are inserted under the presser foot one or two stitches after the previous unit has passed. No threads are cut.

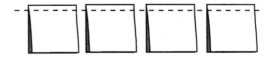

This method saves thread and the time required to start each unit as an individual. It also allows you to repetitively piece the same unit and create a rhythm, thereby reducing mistakes.

Triangle Foundation Paper

Half square triangles are one of the most basic shapes used in quiltmaking. Unfortunately, they are also one of the most often distorted shapes. Gridded triangles have long been present in quilting instructions. Accuracy is greatly increased when half square triangles are pieced using gridded papers. Master triangle foundations may be found on pages 86 and 87. If you would prefer to use commercially prepared papers, refer to the sources listed on page 96, or check with your local quilt shop for availability.

• Photocopy or trace the number of triangle papers necessary for your chosen quilt.

• Cut the fabrics as indicated in the individual pattern. The rectangle or square cut will be slightly larger than the paper foundation.

• Place two fabric pieces right sides together. Position a triangle paper on the wrong side of the light (background) fabric and pin the paper to the fabric pair.

• Starting at the dot, stitch on all dotted lines. Follow the numbered arrows for a continuous seam. Use a small stitch (15 - 20 stitches per inch) and a size 14 sewing machine needle to better perforate the paper foundation.

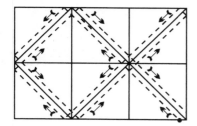

• Cut on all solid lines using a rotary cutter and ruler. Each 6 1/4" pair will yield 8 2" half square triangle units. Each 6 1/4" x 9 1/4" pair will yield 12 2" (finished size) half square triangle units.

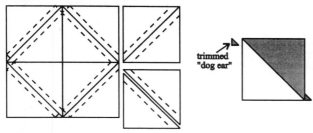

trimmed "dog ear"

• With the paper still attached, press the seam toward the dark fabric.

• Remove the paper foundation. Place your thumb nail on the stitched seam at the center of the block. Pull the paper foundation from the square corner against your thumb nail. This will help to reduce the number of stitches lost at the seam ends.

• Trim all dog ears.

Foundation Paper Piecing

Foundation piecing has been introduced because Whirlpool and Snail's Trail make use of this method. Foundation paper piecing increases accuracy, especially when dealing with small pieces and sharp points.

Points to Remember

•Each master foundation is meant to be used as a pattern to create the foundation papers that you will stitch through. A photocopied foundation may be distorted. Always compare the copy to the master, and make all copies needed from the same machine. If the copy varies significantly from the original, discard the copy and try a different copying machine.

•It is helpful to use a larger sewing machine needle, such as a size 14 needle.

•Stitch with a shorter stitch length, 15 - 20 stitches per inch, to better perforate the paper.

•The lines on the pattern are the actual sewing lines. Sew directly on these lines.

•The fabric pieces will be placed on the **unmarked** side of the foundation paper, and the seam will be sewn from the marked side.

•The fabric pieces do not need to be cut precisely. After stitching, the excess will be trimmed to a 1/4" seam allowance. Take care to allow sufficient fabric to cover the area.

•Each block is diagramed with the numerical sequence of fabric application.

•The foundation pattern will be the mirror image of the final product!!

Foundation Piecing Steps

• Photocopy or trace the foundation piecing designs. If you choose to trace the designs, artist vellum works well.

• Trim away the excess paper from the copied design, leaving 1/4" beyond the outermost line.

• Cut a piece of background fabric for Section 1. The piece should be cut slightly larger than the area, allowing at least 1/4" for the seam allowance on all sides.

•Place the fabric piece against the unmarked side of the foundation paper, position behind Section 1 and pin in place.

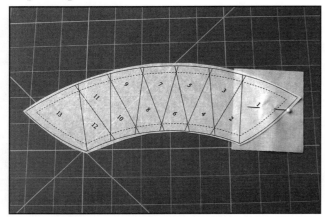

•Flip the assembly to expose the right side of fabric 1 and the unmarked side of the foundation paper.

• Cut a piece of fabric for Section 2. Allow 1/4" for the seam allowance on all sides. Position on top of Section 1 fabric, right sides together (r.s.t.).

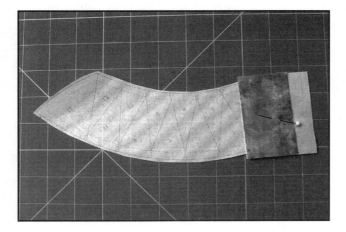

• Flip the paper/fabric assembly over. With the marked side of the foundation facing up, stitch on the seam line between sections 1 and 2. Stitch past the end of the seam line on each end to anchor the fabric. There is no need to back-tack; the stitches are small and will not be pulled out.

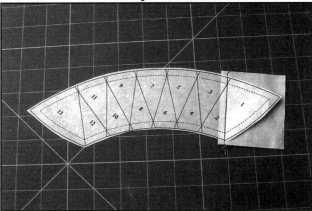

• Finger press the seam to eliminate all pleats or carefully press the seam using an iron without steam. This is a very important step. A poorly pressed seam may mean disaster later.

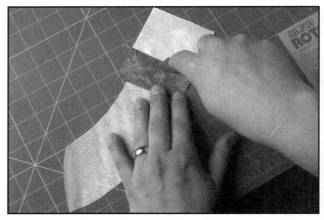

•Flip the paper/fabric assembly over to reveal the printed paper again. Place a postcard along the seam line between Sections 2 and 3.

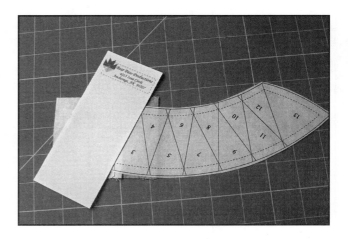

•Fold the paper over this stiff edge and cut away the excess fabric 1/4" from this folded edge. You may use any small ruler with 1/4" markings. I prefer to use an "ADD-A-QUARTER" ruler. The 1/4" wide lip of this ruler fits snuggly against the folded edge giving a consistent 1/4" seam allowance.

•Open the folded paper, and flip again to reveal the fabric pieces. Place fabric 3 in position, raw edges even with the newly cut edge, r.s.t.

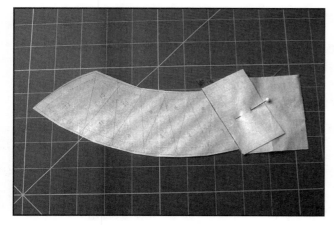

• Continue adding pieces until all sections have been completely covered. Trim the edge of the block along the outermost line, leaving a 1/4" seam allowance.

• After trimming, remove the foundation paper. Pinch the beginning of the seam between the thumb and forefinger of your "wrong" hand and gently pull away the paper, placing all excess force against the thumb nail holding the seam down. If removed in this manner, undue roughness will be reduced and

stretching and pulled stitches will be kept to a minimum.

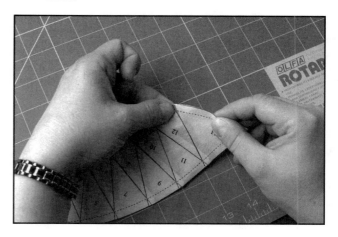

Curved Piecing

To prepare for curved piecing, make plastic templates as directed by the individual pattern. It is helpful to cut the fabric pieces from squares or strips. This will place the grain along the straight edges of the blocks and the bias along the curved edge where it will be the most beneficial.

•Cut the fabric pieces as directed by the individual pattern. Fold the pieces in half and lightly finger crease the center of each curved edge to mark the center of the seam.

• Match the centers of the pieces and pin to anchor. Line up the straight edges and pin at each end.

• Stitch with the concave piece on top. Using a stiletto, or the point of a seam ripper, coax the concave edge into alignment as you stitch a 1/4" seam. Do not stitch more than 1/2" to 1" at a time before you re-align the edges. Press as the pattern directs.

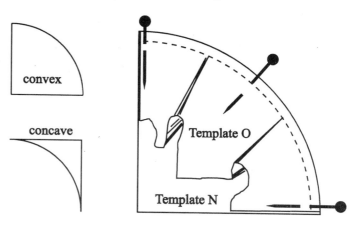

Pin and Match

My personal feeling about pins is that I will use them if only absolutely necessary. In most cases, seams can easily be stitched without the assistance of a pin. At other times, the pinning of seams is a necessary evil. If I feel that pins are important for a particular seam, I will instruct you to pin. The remainder of the time, pinning is up to your personal preference.

Opposing Seams - Generally, methods are employed to ensure that the seams match nicely without the use of pins. This method involves pressing the seams in such a manner that the seams oppose - i.e., the seams are laying in opposite directions. A seam that is pressed in one direction, creates a ridge. When seams oppose, we take advantage of those ridges and make the seams butt up against each other. This will also distribute the bulk of the seam.

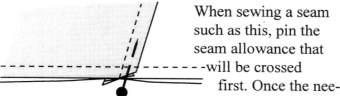

When sewing a seam such as this, pin the seam allowance that will be crossed first. Once the needle has reached the seam allowance, remove the pin. **Do not** sew over pins! The seam should not shift at this point.

Stab Through Pinning - This method is employed when very specific points must match. A pin is "stabbed" through the two points that must match, and anchored. As the units are sewn together, the seam will pass through the point that the pin was securing.

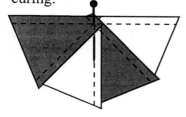
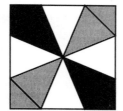

Pressing

Seams are generally pressed toward one side rather than open as in clothing construction. Most often the seam is pressed behind the darker fabric. BUT, all rules are made to be broken!! The instruc-tions given in this book include precise pressing directions, generally in the form of arrows. Care has been taken to ensure that seams oppose if possible, and seam allowances lay behind the darker fabric.

When seams are pressed, first press the seam flat from the wrong side. This smoothes any puckers caused by thread tension problems. Then, open the layers, press from the right side, and watch for any pleating at the seam.

Pressing is a personal topic. Fabric prepared with spray starch can be finger pressed, although I would encourage an occasional trip to the ironing board. Blocks that are steam pressed as they are sewn tend to lay flatter!

Applique

Applique is known among some quilting circles as the "A" word. As a machine piecer, I tend to look for methods that will employ the sewing machine to make my life easier and more efficient.

Applique will be used to stitch the **Hailey's Fan** units to the background fabric. This can be accomplished entirely by machine if desired. The directions given below pertain to machine applique in a general sense. The individual block instructions will detail how the applique technique is to be used.

Machine "Hand" Applique

•Trace and cut applique templates (Hailey's Fan handles for instance) from template plastic. Applique templates **do not** include seam allowances!

•Trace the templates on to the paper side of freezer paper. Cut the freezer paper on the drawn line. It is important to cut the shapes smoothly. You can cut multiple layers of freezer paper at one time. Fan fold the paper and staple the layers together to prevent shifting.

•Place the shiny side of the freezer paper against the right side of the fabric and press in place with an iron on the "wool" setting, this will cause the freezer paper to adhere!

•Cut out the fabric shapes 3/16" (a scant 1/4") larger than the freezer paper. Remove the freezer paper from the right side of the fabric.

•Place the freezer paper, shiny side up, on the wrong side of the cut fabric piece. With the tip of a warm iron, carefully roll the seam allowance over on to the freezer paper template. Press the fabric in place until the seam allowance adheres. This will hold the seam allowance in place until it has been stitched. Fabric sections that will be layered under a second piece of fabric need not be turned under.

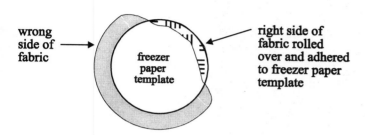

wrong side of fabric →

freezer paper template

right side of fabric rolled over and adhered to freezer paper template

•Glue baste the fabric shapes, with the freezer paper still attached, into place on the background fabric. Roxanne's Glue Baste It works well for this application.

•Machine stitch the pieces in place, using clear .004 nylon thread on top. Practice the stitches described below to determine the one that you prefer.

Blind Hem Stitch	width	1.25
	length	.5
Zig-Zag Stitch	width	1
	length	1

The right swing of the needle is off the edge of the applique and left swing of the needle is fully on the applique fabric.

•Loosen the tension of the top thread to prevent the bobbin thread from popping up to the surface of the background fabric. If this cannot be remedied, match the bobbin thread to the background fabric.

•Use an open toe embroidery foot if available. The open toe allows you to see the needle clearly.

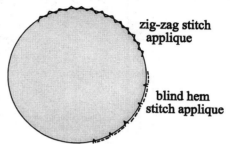

zig-zag stitch applique

blind hem stitch applique

•After all of the applique pieces are stitched in place, and the block is completed, the freezer paper template will need to be removed. Remove the freezer paper by gently tugging at the exposed corner. Care must be taken to prevent loosening of the stitches.

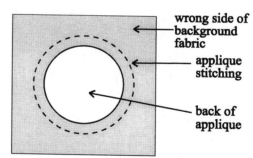

wrong side of background fabric

applique stitching

back of applique

Bride's Bouquet

Fabric Requirements

	Wall Hanging 48" x 48" 5 12" blocks	**Double** 82" x 99" 32 12" blocks
Background	2 1/2 yards	6 1/2 yards
Handle	1/4 yard	1 yard
Buds	1/4 yard	1 yard
Petals (assorted)	3/4 yard	2 3/4 yards
First Border	1/3 yard	1/2 yard
Binding	1/2 yard	1 yard
Backing	3 yards	7 3/4 yards

Cutting Directions

Buds - Yellow	Wall Hanging	Double	
Buds - Yellow			
C - 2 5/8" strips	1 strip	3 strips	
F - 2 5/8" squares	10 squares (1 strip)	64 squares (4 strips)	
Background			
D - 1 3/8" strips	1 strip	6 strips	
E - 1 3/8" x 3 1/2" rectangles	15 (2 strips 1 3/8")	96 (8 strips 1 3/8")	
G - 4 1/4" squares	5 (1 strip)	32 (4 strips)	
I - 3 7/8" squares	5 (1 strip)	32 (4 strips)	
B, Br - 3 3/4" strips	2 strips	6 strips	
Final Border - sides	2 - 6 1/2" x 50"	2 - 6 1/2" x 91 1/2"	
- top and bottom	2 - 6 1/2" x 50"	2 - 6 1/2" x 86 1/2"	
Setting Triangle			
18 1/4" squares	1 square	4 squares (2 strips)	cut twice diagonally
Corner Triangles			
9 3/8" squares	2 squares	2 squares	cut once diagonally
Handle - Green			
A - 6 1/2" strips	1 strip	4 strips	
Petals - Assorted			
H - 3 7/8" squares	30 squares	192 squares	
First Border			
1 1/2" strips	4 strips	8 strips	
Binding			
2 1/2" strips	5 strips	10 strips	

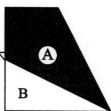

Block Construction

1. Cut handle fabric strips using Template **A**. Cut the number of units listed below.

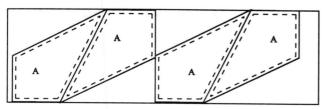

Cut   Wall Hanging 5
Double   32

2. Place the 3 3/4" wide strips of background fabric on the cutting mat **folded wrong sides together**. This will allow you to cut Template **B** and **B-r** at one time. Cut the strips into the number of units listed below.

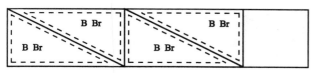

Cut   Wall Hanging 5 B and 5 B-r
Double   32 B and 32 B-r

3. To each Handle **A** stitch a background **B**. Press the seam toward the handle.

4. To the opposite side of Handle **A** stitch a background **Br**. Press the seam toward the handle.

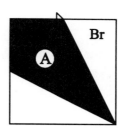

5. Stitch the 2 5/8" bud strip **C**, to the 1 3/8" background strip **D** along the long edge. Press the seam toward the bud fabric. Subcut this strip into 2 5/8" wide pieces as shown below.

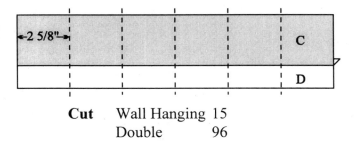

Cut	Wall Hanging	15
	Double	96

6. To one side of this unit, stitch **E** - a 1 3/8" x 3 1/2" background rectangle as shown below. Press the seam toward the bud fabric.

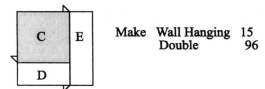

Make Wall Hanging 15
Double 96

7. Cut each 4 1/4" square of background fabric (**G**) twice diagonally to create quarter square triangles.

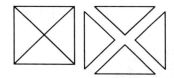

8. To one side of each **F** - a 2 5/8" bud square, stitch a background triangle **G** - a 4 1/4" quarter square triangle. Press seam toward the **F** square.

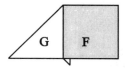

9. Stitch a second background triangle **G** to a second side of the **F** square as shown below. Press this seam toward the square.

Make Wall Hanging 10
Double 64

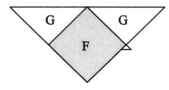

10. Cut each 3 7/8" square of petal and background fabric in half once diagonally.

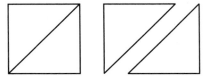

11. Lay out the fabric pieces for each block. The blocks will be sewn one at a time to allow the most variation in fabric placement from one block to the next.

12. Stitch a 3 7/8" half square triangle of petal fabric to each side of the triangle unit from step 9. Press the seams toward the petal fabric. After pressing, be sure to place the resulting unit back in its place among the fabric pieces for that block. This helps prevent "accidental" seams and reverse stitching.

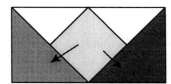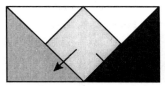

13. Stitch each half square triangle to its appropriate mate, press the seams as indicated in the block diagram below.

14. Assemble the units into sections as shown below. Follow the pressing arrows for the smoothest assembly.

15. Stitch the sections together to form the block. Press as indicated below.   The block will measure 12 1/2" from raw edge to raw edge.

Make Wall Hanging 5 blocks
Double 32 blocks

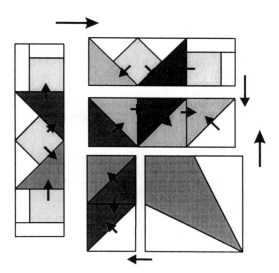

Quilt Top Assembly

1. Assemble the quilt top in diagonal rows as diagramed below.

2. Diagonally piece the first border strips together, cut lengths as needed, and apply to the quilt. Attach the side borders first and then the top and bottom borders. Press seams toward the border strips.

3. Trim final borders to fit and apply to the quilt top. Attach the side borders first, and then the top and bottom borders. Press all seams toward the final border strips.

Buckeye Beauty

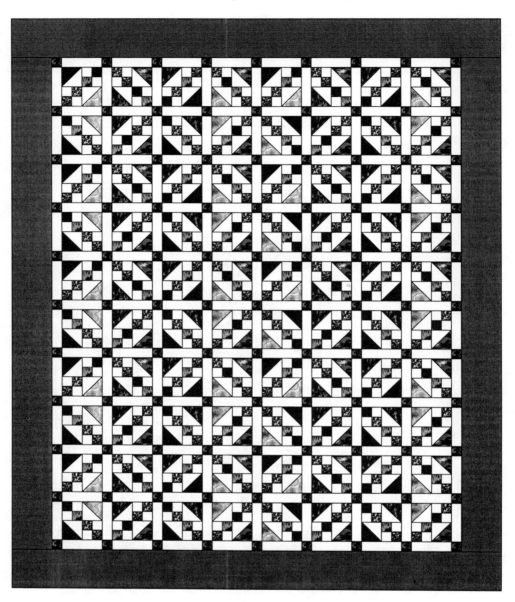

Fabric Requirements

	Twin	Queen
	74" x 94"	94" x 114"
	48 8" blocks	80 8" blocks
Background - includes sashing, may be assorted fabrics or one	4 yards	6 1/4 yards
Dark Colors - assorted	2 yards	3 1/4 yards
Post and Binding	1 1/2 yards	1 3/4 yards
Border - lengthwise grain cut	2 1/2 yards	3 1/8 yards
Backing	5 3/4 yards	8 1/2 yards

Cutting Instructions

	Twin	Queen
Background		
4 7/8" squares	48 (6 strips)	80 (10 strips)
2 1/2" strips	12 (four patches)	20 (four patches)
8 1/2" strips	8 (sashing)	12 (sashing)
Dark Colors		
4 7/8" squares	48 (6 strips)	80 (10 strips)
2 1/2" strips	12 (four patches)	20(four patches)
Posts and Binding		
2 1/2" strips	5 (posts)	7 (posts)
2 1/2"strips	9 (binding)	11(binding)
Final Border - sides	2 - 6 1/2" x 86"	2 - 6 1/2" x 106"
- top and bottom	2 - 6 1/2" x 78"	2 - 6 1/2" x 98"

Four Patch Units

1. Stitch each 2 1/2"-wide dark strip to a 2 1/2"-wide background strip along the long edge. Press the seam toward the dark strip. Repeat with all 2 1/2"-wide dark strips.

2. Place two sets of sewn strips right sides together, reversing the colors as shown in the diagram below. The seam allowances will be opposing.

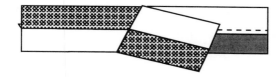

3. Trim the selvage from the strip ends. Cut the strip pairs into 2 1/2" segments.

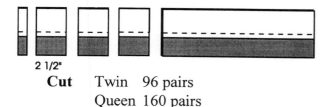

2 1/2"

Cut	Twin	96 pairs
	Queen	160 pairs

4. Chain piece the subcut pairs. The pairs are cut with the seam allowances aligned and ready for stitching. Press the seam to one side. Each four patch unit will measure 4 1/2" from edge to edge.

Half Square Triangle Units

1. Cut each 4 7/8" square of dark and background fabric in half once diagonally.

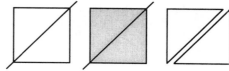

2. Stitch each dark 4 7/8" half square triangle to a background triangle. Press the seam toward the dark triangle. Trim all dog ears.

Block Assembly

1. Stitch each four patch to a half square triangle unit. Note the placement of the dark fabric pieces. Press the seam toward the half square triangle unit.

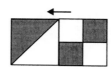

2. Stitch units from step 1 (above) together. Press the long seam in one direction. Each block will measure 8 1/2" from raw edge to raw edge.

Sashing and Post Construction

1. Stitch 2 1/2"-wide post strips to 8 1/2"-wide sashing strips along the long edge. Press the seam toward the sashing strip.

Make Twin   4
　　　　Queen 6

2. Trim the selvage from the strip end. Subcut each sewn strip into 2 1/2"-wide segments.

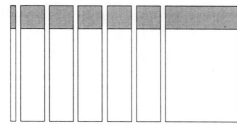

Cut Twin   54
　　　Queen 88

3. Cut the remaining 8 1/2"-wide sashing strips into 2 1/2" segments.

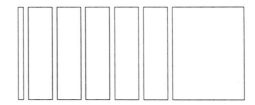

Cut Twin   56
　　　Queen 90

4. Cut the remaining 2 1/2"-wide post strip into 2 1/2" squares.

Cut Twin   9
　　　Queen 11

Quilt Top Assembly

1. Join blocks and sashing strips together into rows. Press all seams toward sashing strips.

2. Join sashing/post units together into rows. Add a single post to the end of each row. Press all seams toward the sashing strips.

3. Assemble rows of blocks with rows of sashing between them. Press the long seams toward the sashing strips.

4. Trim final borders to fit and apply to the quilt top. Attach side borders first and then the top and bottom borders. Press all seams toward the final border.

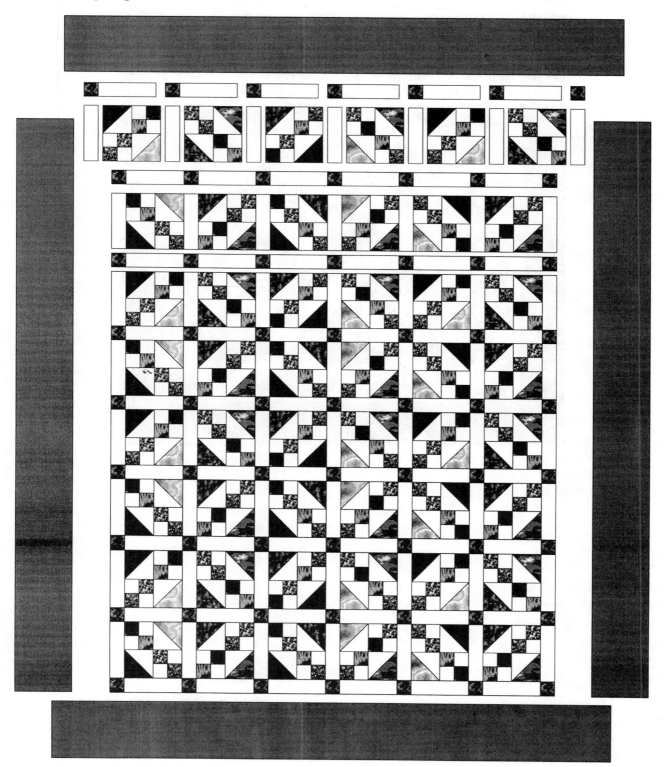

Twin Size Quilt Diagramed

Flannel Star

Fabric Requirements

	Wall Hanging	**Double**
	84" square	84" x 106"
	9 22 1/2" blocks	12 22 1/2" blocks
Assorted Darks - small triangles	1 3/4 yards	2 yards
Assorted Plaids - large triangles and squares	1 3/4 yards	2 yards
Background	3 3/4 yards	4 1/2 yards
First Border	1/2 yard	1/2 yard
Final Border	2 1/2 yards	3 yards
Backing	5 yards	7 3/4 yards
Binding	3/4 yards	1 yard

Cutting Directions

NOTE each 22 1/2" block requires 4 squares 5 3/8" plus 1 square 8" of matching plaid fabric; and 6 squares 5" plus 8 squares 2 3/8" of matching dark fabric. Please cut your fabric accordingly.

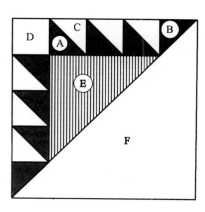

		Wall Hanging	Double
Dark - Assorted			
A	5" squares	54 (7 strips)	72 (9 strips)
B	2 3/8" squares	72 (5 strips)	96 (6 strips)
Background			
C	5" squares	54 (7 strips)	72 (9 strips)
D	2" squares	72 (4 strips)	96 (5 strips)
F	8 3/8" squares	36 (8 strips)	48 (10 strips)
Plaid - Assorted			
E	5 3/8" squares	36 (6 strips)	48 (7 strips)
G	8" squares	9 (2 strips)	12 (3 strips)
First Border			
1 1/2" strips		7 strips	8 strips
Final Border - sides		2 - 7 1/2" x 74"	2 - 7 1/2" x 96"
		2 - 7 1/2" x 88"	2 - 7 1/2" x 88"
Binding - 2 1/2" strips		9 strips	10 strips

Block Construction

NOTE The fabrics have been cut to allow for the use of triangle foundation papers when constructing half square triangles. If you wish to piece the triangles in the traditional method (triangle to triangle), cut each 5" square into four 2 3/8" squares and cut each 2 3/8" square once diagonally. Each square will produce eight half square triangles 2 3/8".

1. Photocopy or trace the number of triangle foundation papers (found on page 87) necessary for your chosen quilt. The paper used will be two squares long by two squares wide.

      Copy Wall Hanging 54
              Double   72

2. Place a 5" square of background fabric (**C**) right sides together with a 5" square of dark fabric (**A**). Construct half square triangles following the triangle foundation paper method detailed on page 12. Each square pair will yield eight half square triangle units measuring 2" raw edge to raw edge.

3. Cut each 2 3/8" dark square (**B**) in half once diagonally.

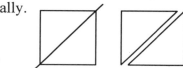

4. Stitch pairs of three half square triangle units together as shown. Press the seams toward the darker fabric as indicated by the arrows. Each block will require 8 pairs.

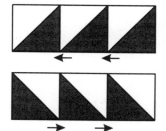

Make
Wall Hanging   72 pairs
Double   96 pairs

5. To one end of each strip add a triangle **B**. Press the seam toward the triangle **B**. One strip of each pair will also receive a background square **D**. Press this seam toward background square **D**.

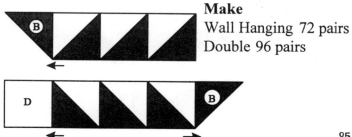

Make
Wall Hanging 72 pairs
Double 96 pairs

6. Stitch the shorter half square triangle strip to a plaid half square triangle (**E**). Press this seam toward **E** as indicated by the arrow. Attach the remaining half square triangle strip to the adjacent edge. Press this seam toward **E** also. Handle these units with care due to the long, unstabilized bias edge.

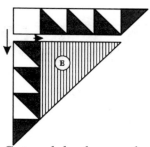

Make
Wall Hanging 72
Double   96

7. Cut each background square **F** once diagonally. Attach the background half square triangle (**F**) to the bias edge of the unit from step 6. Press the seam toward **F**. This unit, sometimes call a Delectable Mountain, will measure 8" from raw edge to raw edge.

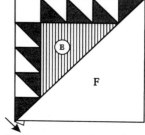

8. Using 8 units from step 7, and one plaid square **G**, assemble the block as shown below. Press the seams as indicated. Pressing the seams in this manner will allow the blocks to be turned alternately creating opposing seams.

Make   Wall Hanging 9 blocks
                  Double   12 blocks

Quilt Top Assembly

1. Stitch the quilt top together into rows, and sew the rows together to form the quilt top: wall hanging - 3 x 3, and double - 3 x 4.

2. Diagonally piece the first border, and cut lengths as needed. Attach side borders first and then the top and bottom border. Press all seams toward the border strips.

3. Trim final borders to fit and apply to the quilt top. Attach side borders first and then the top and bottom border strips. Press all seams toward the final border strips.

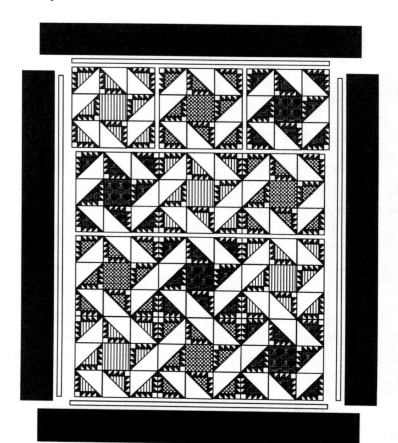

The Delectable Mountain quilt block is a lot of fun to play with!! The fact that it is basically a large half square triangle allows you to place it in the same ways. Most any block pattern constructed of half square triangles can be translated into a quilt top using Delectable Mountain blocks. Another source of inspiration might be a good Log Cabin setting book.

The Delectable Mountain block can also be mixed with plain blocks as in the Flannel Star - increasing the possibilities for its use. So, when you are ready to set the smaller blocks together into the Flannel Star blocks, try your own setting first. I bet you will find one that you like just as much.

The quilt designs below demonstrate a few additional ways to set the blocks. Use your imagination to design your own quilt.

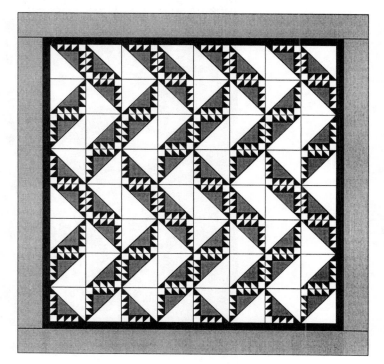

Old Maid's Puzzle

Fabric Requirements

	Twin 68" x 84" 48 8" blocks	**Queen** 84" x 100" 80 8" blocks
Background - black - includes all piecing, borders and binding	7 yards	9 1/2 yards
Bright Colors - assorted	3 yards	4 1/2 yards
Backing	5 1/4 yards	7 3/4 yards

Cutting Instructions

NOTE Each pair of two blocks requires: Background: 1 rectangle 6 1/4" x 9 1/4", 8 squares 2 1/2" and 4 rectangles 2 1/2" x 3 1/4"; and Bright Color: 1 rectangle 6 1/4" x 9 1/4" and 2 squares 4 7/8". Please cut your fabric accordingly.

	Twin	Queen
Background		
6 1/4" x 9 1/4" rectangles	24 (6 strips 6 1/4")	40 (10 strips 6 1/4")
2 1/2" squares	192 (12 strips)	320 (20 strips)
2 1/2" x 3 1/4" rectangles	96 (6 strips 3 1/4")	160 (10 strips 3 1/4")
Pieced Border		
6 1/4" x 9 1/4" rectangles	5 (2 strips 6 1/4")	7 (2 strips 6 1/4")
4 7/8" squares	30 (4 strips)	38 (5 strips)
4 1/2" squares	4	4
First Border	6 strips 2 1/2"	8 strips 2 1/2"
Final Border - sides	2 - 4 1/2" x 80"	2 - 4 1/2" x 96"
- top and bottom	2 - 4 1/2" x 72"	2 - 4 1/2" x 88"
Binding	8 strips 2 1/2"	10 strips 2 1/2"
Bright Colors		
6 1/4" x 9 1/4" rectangles	24 assorted rectangles	40 assorted rectangles
4 7/8" squares	48 assorted squares	80 assorted squares
Pieced Border	5 rectangles 6 1/4" x 9 1/4"	7 rectangles 6 1/4" x 9 1/4"
	60 rectangles 2 1/2" x 3 1/4"	76 rectangles 2 1/2" x 3 1/4"

Half Square Triangle Construction

NOTE The fabrics have been cut to allow for the use of triangle foundation papers when constructing half square triangles. If you wish to piece the triangles in the traditional method (triangle to triangle), cut each 6 1/4" x 9 1/4" rectangle into six 2 7/8" squares and cut each 2 7/8" square once diagonally. Each rectangle will produce twelve half square triangles 2 7/8".

1. Photocopy or trace the number of triangle foundation papers (found on page 86) necessary for your chosen quilt. The paper used will be three squares long by two squares wide.

Copy	Twin	24
	Queen	40

2. Place a 6 1/4" x 9 1/4" rectangle of background fabric right sides together with a 6 1/4" x 9 1/4" rectangle of colored fabric. Construct half square triangles following the triangle foundation paper method detailed on the paper. Each rectangle will yield twelve half square triangle units measuring 2 1/2", enough units for two Old Maid's Puzzle blocks.

Grandmother's Choice Unit

This little trick was taught to me by Debbie Caffrey. Two half square triangle units are each sewn to a rectangle. The two resulting units are sewn together, and subcut - creating two identical Grandmother's Choice units. This greatly speeds piecing of this versatile unit.

NOTE Each block requires 2 grandmother's choice units as constructed above. Use 4 half square triangle units from each colored 6 1/4" x 9 1/4" rectangle to make 4 grandmother's choice units which will be enough units for 2 blocks.

1. Stitch **4** half square triangle units each to a 2 1/2" x 3 1/4" rectangle of background fabric. Press the seam toward the rectangle.

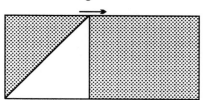

2. Stitch two units together. Match the raw edges. The seams **will not match.**

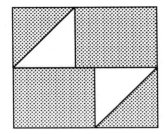

3. Carefully snip the seam allowance through the seam line at the center of the long seam. This will allow the seam allowance to be split and pressed in two different directions. Split the seam and press the seams toward the triangles.

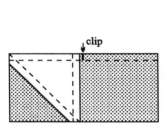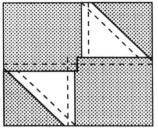

4. Place the pressed unit, right side up, on the cutting mat. Align the **Omnigrid #96** ruler as diagramed below. Line up the 4" ruler marking with the left edge of the pieced unit. The 1 3/4" ruling will fall along the center seam, and the point of the ruler will extend past the fabric edge, allowing the "nub" line to align with the edge. Cut the pieced unit along the diagonal edge of the ruler, creating two identical grandmother's choice units. **Template C** has been provided if you do not have access to the **Omnigrid #96** ruler.

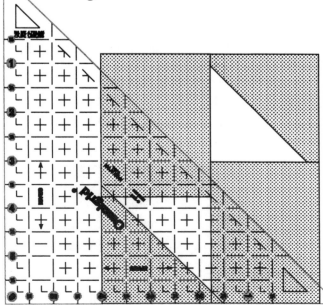

Block Construction

1. Cut each 4 7/8" square of colored fabric in half once diagonally.

2. To each grandmother's choice unit, stitch a matching 4 7/8" half square triangle of colored fabric. You are stitching bias to bias. Take extra care so that you do not stretch the fabric. Press the seam toward the triangle. Make 2 units for each block.

Make
Twin   96
Queen   160

3. To each half square triangle unit remaining (8 from each 6 1/4" x 9 1/4" rectangle) stitch a 2 1/2" square of background fabric. Press the seam toward the background square.

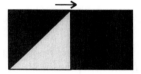

Make
Twin   192
Queen   320

4. Pair the units from step 3. Stitch and press the seam as indicated. Make 2 for each block.

Make
Twin   96
Queen   160

5. Stitch the units together to create the block. Press. This completed unit will measure 8 1/2".

Make
Twin   48
Queen   80

Pieced Border Construction

1. Construct half square triangle units using foundation triangle papers as detailed earlier. If you prefer, the 6 1/4" x 9 1/4" rectangles of fabric may be cut into triangles for the standard piecing method. Each background fabric/colored fabric pair will yield 12 half square triangle units.

2. Construct grandmother's choice units using half square triangle units and **colored 2 1/2" x 3 1/4" rectangles.** Watch the diagram below closely when constructing border units. The color placement is reverse that of the block unit.

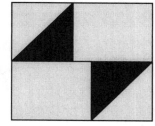

3. Cut each 4 7/8" square of background fabric in half once diagonally.

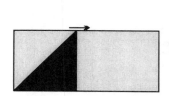

4. Stitch a background 4 7/8" triangle to each grandmother's choice unit. Press the seam toward the background triangle.

Make
  Twin 60
  Queen 76

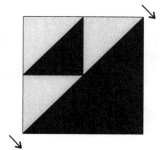

5. Stitch together the pieced border units. Follow the diagram below.

Sides Twin - 8 units on each side of the 4" square of background fabric
        Queen - 10 units on each side of the 4" square

Top and Bottom
    Twin - 7 units on each side of the 4" square
    Queen - 9 units on each side of the 4" square

Twin Borders
Top/Bottom   Sides

Queen Borders
Top/Bottom   Sides

Quilt Top Assembly

1. Stitch the quilt top together into rows, and sew the rows together to form the quilt top: twin - 6 x 8, and queen - 8 x 10.

2. Diagonally piece the first border, and cut lengths as needed. Attach side borders first and then the top and bottom borders. Press all seams toward the first border.

3. Stitch the pieced borders in place. Attach the side borders first and then the top and bottom borders. Press all seams toward the first border.

4. Trim final borders to fit and apply to the quilt top. Attach side borders first and then the top and bottom border strips. Press all seams toward the final border strips.

Twin Size Quilt Diagram

Churn Dash Garden

Fabric Requirements

	Lap 64" x 86" 8 12" blocks	**Queen** 86" x 108" 18 12" blocks
Background	3 1/2 yards	5 1/4 yards
Assorted Dark Colors	1 yard	1 3/4 yards
Sashing, First Border **and Binding**	2 yards	3 1/4 yards
Final Border	2 1/2 yards	3 yards
Backing	5 1/4 yards	7 3/4 yards

Cutting Instructions

	Lap	Queen
Background		
4 7/8" squares	16 (2 strips)	36 (5 strips)
2 1/2" x 21" strips	8 strips	18 strips
4 1/2" squares	8 (1 strip)	18 (2 strips)
Sashing		
2 3/4" strips	8 strips	16 strips

After cutting all of the pieces listed above, Cut the **S**etting Triangles, **C**orner Triangles, and **P**osts from the remaining yardage.

	Lap	Queen
Setting Triangles		
23 1/2" squares	2 squares	3 squares
Corner Triangles		
14 5/8" squares	2 squares	2 squares
Posts		
3 1/2" squares	17 squares	31 squares
Assorted Dark Colors		
4 7/8" squares	16 squares	36 squares
2 1/2" x 21" strips	8 strips	18 strips
Sashing, First Border, and Binding		
Sashing - 1 3/4" strips	16 strips	32 strips
Posts - 1 3/4" strips	6 strips	11 strips
First Border - 1 1/2" strips	7 strips	9 strips
Binding - 2 1/2" strips	8 strips	10 strips
Final Border - sides	2 - 6 1/2" x 79"	2 - 6 1/2" x 100"
- top and bottom	2 - 6 1/2" x 90"	2 - 6 1/2" x 90"

Block Construction

1. Cut each 4 7/8" square of Background and Dark Color fabric in half once diagonally. Stitch each Dark Color 4 7/8" half square triangle to a Background fabric triangle. Press the seam toward the Dark Color fabric. Trim all dog ears. Make 4 matching half square triangle units for each block.

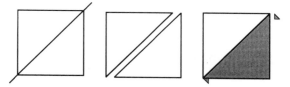

2. Stitch each 2 1/2" x 21" strip of Background fabric to a 2 1/2" x 21" strip of Dark Color fabric. Press the seam toward the Dark fabric.

4. Subcut each sewn strip into 4 squares 4 1/2".

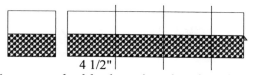

4 1/2"

5. Construct the blocks using the pieced units and the 4 1/2" squares of background fabric. Press the seams as indicated by the arrows.

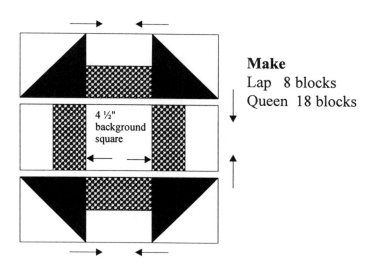

4 1/2"
background
square

Make
Lap 8 blocks
Queen 18 blocks

Sashing and Post Construction

1. Stitch a 1 1/4" strip of sashing fabric to each side of a 2 3/4" strip of background fabric. Press the seams toward the sashing fabric.

2. Cut the sewn strips into 12 1/2" lengths.

← 12 1/2" →

Cut Lap 24
Queen 48

3. Photocopy or trace the post foundation at the right.
Copy Lap 17 of each unit
Queen 31 of each unit

4. Cut each 3 1/2" square of background fabric twice diagonally. Cut the 1 3/4" strips of post fabric into lengths (1 - 6 1/4" piece, and 2 - 3" pieces per post) for paper piecing.

5. Paper piece the units following the paper piecing directions found on page 12. Trim on the outer solid line and remove the paper foundation.

6. Stitch each Unit A to a Unit B. Press the seam toward the dark fabric.

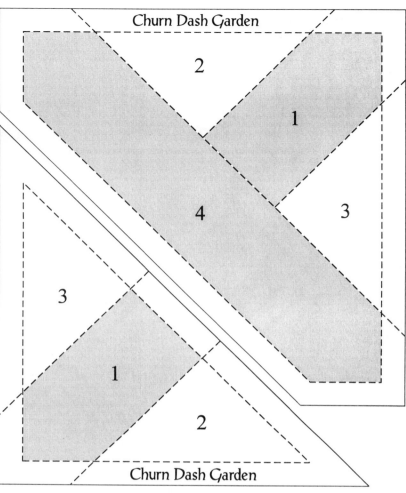

Churn Dash Garden

Churn Dash Garden

Quilt Top Assembly

1. Lay the quilt top out on a floor or design wall. The blocks will be assembled in diagonal rows. It is also helpful to lay out the setting and corner triangles. The setting triangles are easy to rotate into an incorrect position. Join blocks and sashing strips together into rows. Press all seams toward sashing strips.

2. Join sashing and post units together into rows. Press all seams toward the sashing strips.

3. Stitch a row of block/sashing to a row of sashing/post. Press the long seam toward the sashing/post strip.

4. Following the diagram closely, stitch setting triangles to each end of the unit. Press the seams toward the triangles.

5. Continue to assemble the quilt top in this manner. Attach the corner triangles last.

6. Diagonally piece the first border strips together, cut lengths as needed, and apply to the quilt. Attach the side borders first and then the top and bottom borders. Press seams toward the border strips.

7. Trim final borders to fit and apply to the quilt top, attach side borders first and then the top and bottom borders. Press all seams toward the final border.

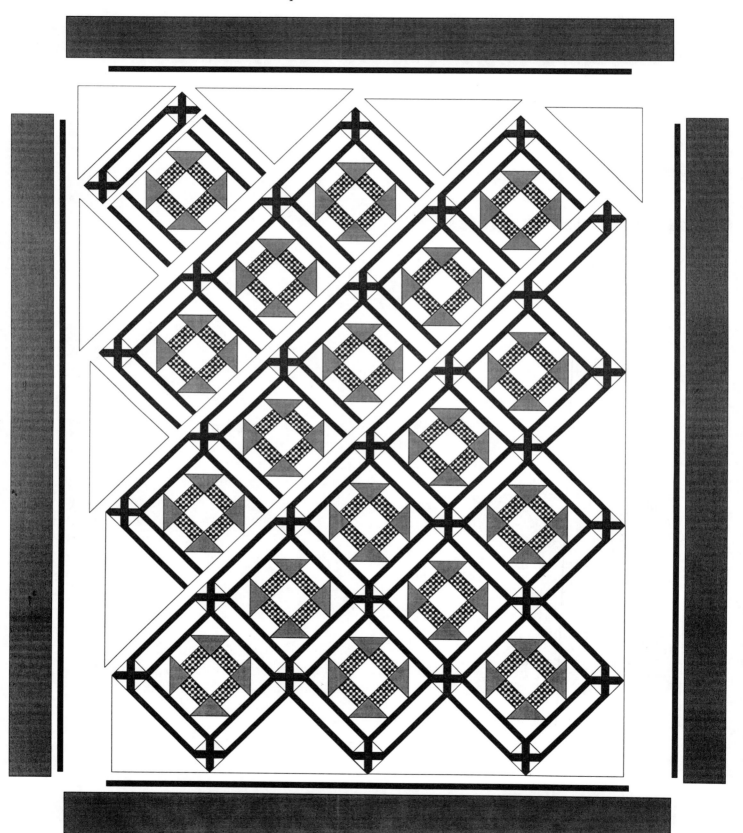

Deb's Star

Fabric Requirements

	Lap 69" x 81" 20 12" blocks	**Double** 81" x 93" 30 12" blocks
Black	1 1/4 yards	1 3/4 yards
White	1 1/4 yards	1 3/4 yards
Star —Dark	2 yards	2 3/4 yards
Star — Medium	1 1/2 yards	2 1/4 yards
First Border	1/2 yard	3/4 yard
Final Border	2 1/4 yards	2 1/2 yards
Binding	3/4 yard	3/4 yard
Backing	5 1/4 yards	6 yards

Cutting Instructions

NOTE Each block requires: Dark - 2 squares 5 1/4" and 2 squares 4 7/8" of matching fabric, and Medium - 2 squares 4 7/8" and 1 square 5 1/4" of a coordinating fabric. Please cut your fabric accordingly.

	1 Block	Lap	Double
Black			
1 15/16" strips	1/2 strip	8 strips	12 strips
White			
1 15/16" strips	1/2 strip	8 strips	12 strips
Star — Dark			
A - 5 1/4" squares	2 squares	40 squares	60 squares
B - 4 7/8" squares	2 squares	40 squares	60 squares
Star — Medium			
C - 4 7/8" squares	2 squares	40 squares	60 squares
D - 5 1/4" squares	1 square	20 squares	30 squares
First Border			
2" strips		6 strips	7 strips
Checkerboard Border —Black			
2" strips		9 strips	10 strips
Checkerboard Border — White			
2" strips		9 strips	10 strips
Final Border - sides		2 - 6 1/2" x 73"	2 - 6 1/2" x 85"
- top and bottom		2 - 6 1/2" x 75"	2 - 6 1/2" x 85"

Block Construction

1. Stitch black and cream 1 15/16" wide strips together as diagramed below. Press the seams toward the black strips. Subcut the sewn strip into units 1 15/16" wide. Each strip will yield 11 units.

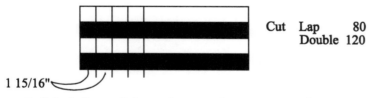

1 15/16"

Cut   Lap   80
      Double 120

2. Stitch four of the units together to create the sixteen patch center square. Press the long seams in one direction.

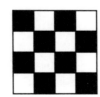

Make   Lap   20
       Double 30

3. Cut each **B** and C square (4 7/8" squares) once diagonally to create half square triangles.

4. Cut each **A** and **D** square (5 1/4" squares) twice diagonally to create quarter square triangles.

5. Stitch each **B** half square triangle to a **C** half square triangle, right sides together. Press the seams toward the dark fabric. Trim the dog ears.

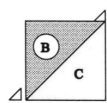

make 4 for each block

6. Stitch each medium quarter square triangle **D** to a dark quarter square triangle **A**. Position the triangles as diagramed below, stitch two of each combination. Press the seam toward the dark fabric. Trim the dog ears.

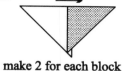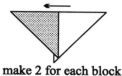

make 2 for each block   make 2 for each block

7. To each medium side of two of the half square triangle units from step **5**, stitch a quarter square triangle **A**. Fold each unit in half and finger press to crease alignment marks on each of the units. Carefully press the seam toward the dark triangle.

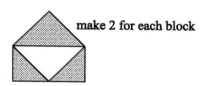

make 2 for each block

8. To the two remaining half square triangle units from step **5**, apply a unit from step **6**. Align square corners, be sure to line up the opposing seams. Stitch from square corner to the point of the triangle. Press the seams toward the dark fabric.

make 2 for each block

9. Assemble the block as diagramed, take care to match the seam. Press the seams away from the sixteen patch unit.

Make Lap   20
Double 30

Pieced Border Construction

1. Stitch each 2"-wide white strip to a 2" wide black strip along the long edge. Press the seam toward the black strip. Repeat with all pieced border strips.

2. Stitch strip pairs together into larger strip unit. Press all seams toward the black strips.

3. Straighten the strip end. Cut the strip units into 2" segments.

cut into 2" segments

4. Stitch the 2" segments together into long chains. "Break" the long chain apart between squares, by removing stitches, to create strips of the correct length to border your quilt. Make 4 strips of the length specified for your side borders and 4 strips for the top and bottom borders.

Side Borders:
Lap - 21 black and 21 white squares
Double - 25 black and 25 white squares

Top and Bottom Borders:
Lap - 18 black and 18 white squares
Double - 23 black and 23 white squares

5. Stitch strips into pairs. Alternate the placement of the black and white squares to create a checkerboard effect.

Quilt Top Assembly

1. Stitch the blocks together into rows, and sew the rows together to form the quilt top:
lap - 4 x 5; and double - 5 x 6.

2. Diagonally piece the first border, and cut lengths as needed. Attach side borders first and then the top and bottom borders. Press the seams toward the border strips.

3. Add the pieced border strips. Attach the side borders first and then the top and bottom border strips. Press the seams toward the first border.

4. Trim final borders to fit and apply to the quilt top. Attach side borders first and then the top and bottom borders. Press all seams toward the final border strips.

NOTE If you choose to use a pieced final border, cut assorted strips 6 1/2" wide. Piece strips together diagonally before trimming border strips to length and applying to the quilt top.

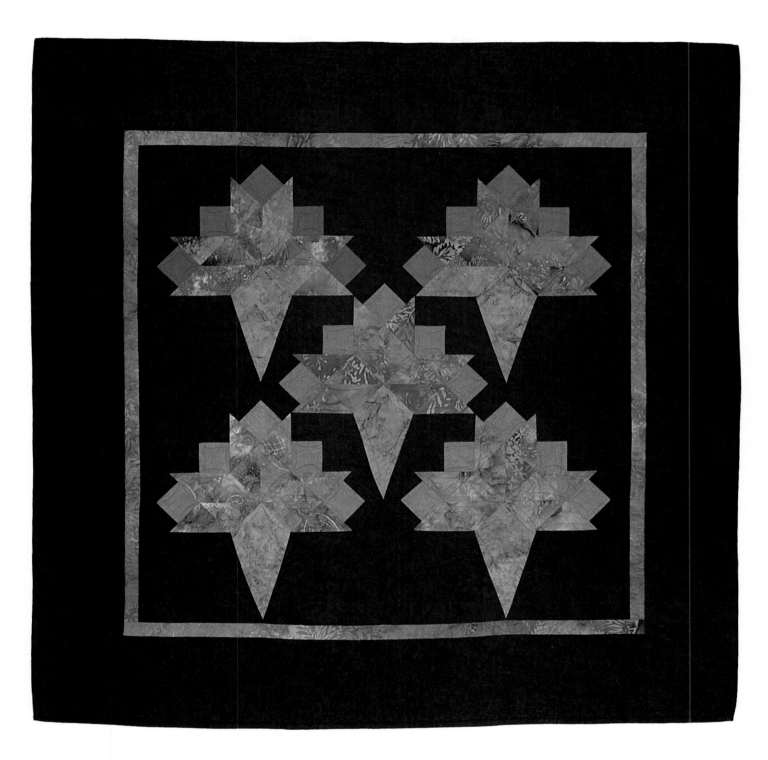

Bride's Bouquet, by Brenda Henning, 1996; Anchorage, AK;
48" x 48". Quilted by Brenda Henning. Photo: Randy Brandon.

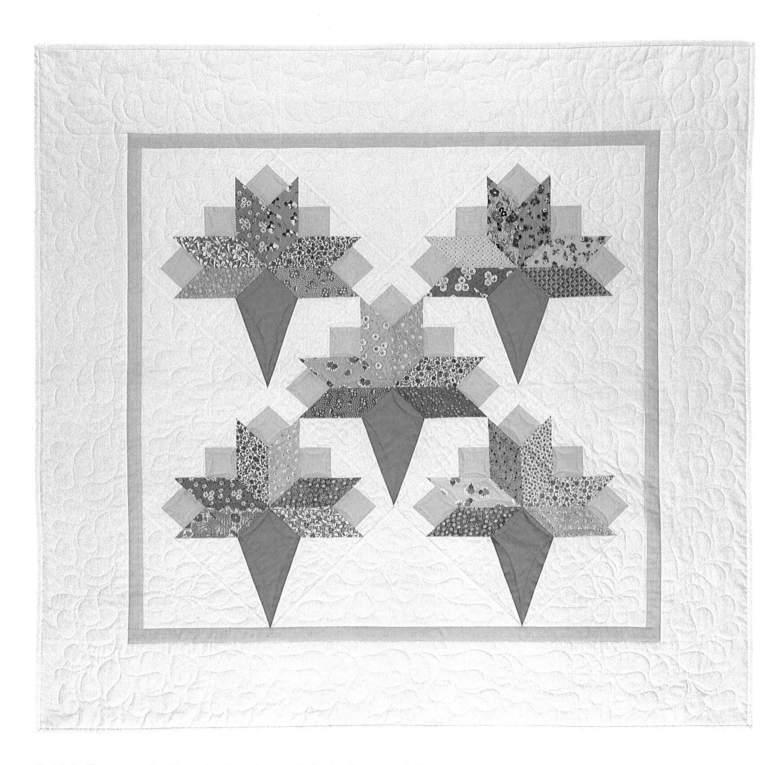

Bride's Bouquet, by Brenda Henning, 1996; Anchorage, AK;
48" x 48". Quilted by Norma Kindred. Photo: Randy Brandon.

Buckeye Beauty, by Brenda Henning, 1998; Anchorage, AK; 94" x 114". Quilted by Norma Kindred. Photo: Randy Brandon.

Flannel Star, by Brenda Henning, 1996; Anchorage, AK;
84" x 84". Quilted by Norma Kindred. Photo: Randy Brandon.

Old Maid's Puzzle, by Brenda Henning, 1998; Anchorage, AK; 84" x 100". Quilted by Norma Kindred. Photo: Randy Brandon.

Churn Dash Garden, by Brenda Henning, 1993; Anchorage, AK; 86" x 108". Quilted by Norma Kindred. Photo: Randy Brandon. The blocks for this quilt were won in a drawing at a local quilt shop. The floral fabric was provided to each participant to be used as the focus fabric.

Deb's Star, by Debbie Repasky, with help from the Sourdough Stitchers, 1997; Anchorage, AK; 81" x 93". Quilted by Norma Kindred. Photo: Randy Brandon. Fabric selection was to include a light and a dark of the same color family. What a wonderful range of fabrics! No one knew what the other girls had selected.

Whirlpool, by Brenda Henning, 1995; Anchorage, AK;
56" x 56". Quilted by Norma Kindred. Photo: Randy Brandon.

Snail's Trail, by Debbie Repasky, with help from the Sourdough Stitchers, 1997; Anchorage, AK; 56" x 72". Quilted by Norma Kindred. Photo: Randy Brandon.

Hailey's Fan, by Brenda Henning, 1998; Anchorage, AK; 94" x 106". Quilted by Norma Kindred.
Photo: Randy Brandon. This quilt is in the collection of Hailey Ann Fanning.

Hailey's Fan, by Pam Ventgen , 1998; Anchorage, AK. Quilted by Pam Ventgen. Photo: Randy Brandon. Yet another possible setting for these dynamic blocks. Beautiful!

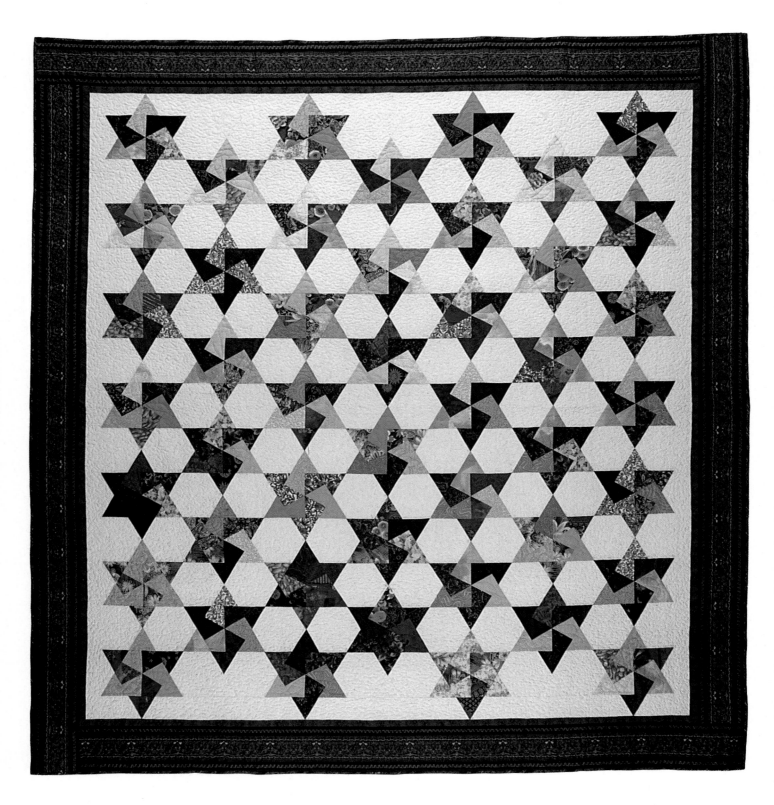

Puzzling Hexes, by Brenda Henning, 1995; Anchorage, AK;
92" x 98". Quilted by Norma Kindred. Photo: Randy Brandon.

Scrap Hunter, by Brenda Henning, 1997; Anchorage, AK;
86" x 104". Quilted by Norma Kindred. Photo: Randy Brandon.

Scrap Hunter, by Brenda Henning, 1996; Anchorage, AK;
68" x 68". Quilted by Brenda Henning. Photo: Randy Brandon.

Drunkard's Path, by Diana Bradley, 1998; Anchorage, AK; 81" x 93". Quilted by Loretta Tibor.
Photo: Randy Brandon. Fabulous use of fabric!

Antique Drunkard's Path, quilt maker and date unknown. 70" x 78". Photo: Randy Brandon.
Shown as a layout possibility, no diagram is given.

Whirlpool

Fabric Requirements

Wall Hanging
56" square
6" blocks

Background	2 1/4 yards
Darkest	1 yard
Medium Dark	1/2 yard
Medium	2/3 yard
Medium Light	1/2 yard
Light	1/3 yard
First Border	1/4 yard
Final Border	1 3/4 yards
Backing	3 1/2 yards
Binding	1/2 yard

Cutting Instructions

The Log Cabin blocks will be pieced in the traditional manner, the logs will be cut to the exact size before piecing. I find that this gives the most consistent results. The Reel blocks are pieced on a paper foundation. This gives perfect, square blocks every time.

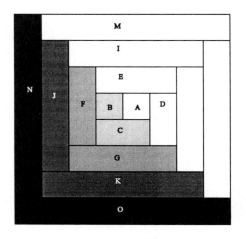

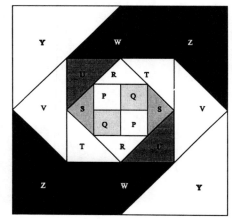

	# of Strips	Subcut into	Special Directions
Light			
B	2 strips 1 1/4"	16 - 1 1/4" squares	
C		16 - 1 1/4" x 2"	
Q	3 strips 1 1/2"	66 - 1 1/2" squares	
Medium Light			
F	3 strips 1 1/4"	16 - 1 1/4" x 2 3/4"	
G		16 - 1 1/4" x 3 1/2"	
S	3 strips 2 1/2"	33 - 2 1/2" squares	cut once diagonally
Medium			
J	4 strips 1 1/4"	16 - 1 1/4" x 4 1/4"	
K		16 - 1 1/4" x 5"	
U	3 strips 3"	3 - 3" squares	cut once diagonally
Medium Dark			
W	3 strips 3 1/2"	33 - 3 1/2" squares	cut once diagonally
Dark			
N	5 strips 1 1/4"	16 - 1 1/4" x 5 3/4"	
O		16 - 1 1/4" x 6 1/2"	
Z	4 strips 4 1/2"	33 - 4 1/2" squares	cut once diagonally
Background			
A	12 strips 1 1/4"	16 - 1 1/4" squares	
D		16 - 1 1/4" x 2"	
E		16 - 1 1/4" x 2 3/4"	
H		16 - 1 1/4" x 3 1/2"	
I		16 - 1 1/4" x 4 1/4"	
L		16 - 1 1/4" x 5"	
M		16 - 1 1/4" x 5 3/4"	
P	3 strips 1 1/2"	66 - 1 1/2" squares	
R	3 strips 2 1/2"	33 - 2 1/2" squares	cut once diagonally
T	3 strips 3"	33 - 3" squares	cut once diagonally
V	3 strips 3 1/2"	33 - 3 1/2" squares	cut once diagonally
Y	4 strips 4 1/2"	33 - 4 1/2" squares	cut once diagonally
First Border			
	5 strips 1 1/2"		crossgrain cut
Final Border			
sides		2 strips 6 1/2" x 50"	lengthwise cut
top and bottom		2 strips 6 1/2" x 64"	lengthwise cut
Binding			
	6 strips 2 1/2"		

Log Cabin Block Construction

NOTE Accuracy is very important to the success of any log cabin project.

- All logs have been cut to the correct size. If stitched correctly, there will be no excess strip, and there will be no need to stretch the log to fit.
- If you are having difficulty making the logs fit:
  a) double check your seam allowance; and
  b) double check your cutting accuracy.

1. Stitch all **A** and **B** 1 1/4" squares together. Chain piece as you stitch the log cabin units to save time and thread. Press the seam toward the **B** square, which is dark.

2. Stitch all **C** rectangles to the unit from step 1 above. Press the seam toward the **C** rectangle.

3. Continue adding rectangles to the log cabin in the alphabetic order listed in the cutting directions. Press all seams toward the outer edge of the block.

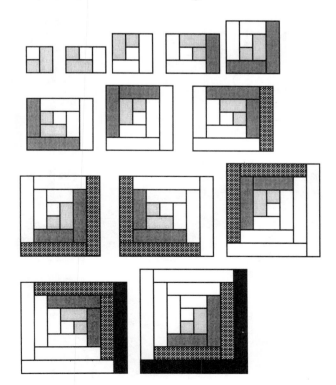

Reel Block Construction

1. Photocopy or trace the Reel foundation (found on page 88) 33 times.

2. Stitch each **P** - 1 1/2" background square - to a **Q** - a light 1 1/2" square. Press each seam toward the darker fabric. Stitch each pair to another pair - alternating the darker square - to create 33 "4-patch" blocks.

3. Paper piece the Reel blocks using the 4-patch unit from step 2 above as the center. Refer to the foundation paper **P/Q** designation for the 4-patch placement. The sizes given in the cutting instructions are oversized for ease of assembly. Follow the paper piecing instructions given on pages 11 - 13 to create 33 reel blocks.

4. Trim the pieced unit on the solid line, this will leave a 1/4" seam allowance at the edge of the reel block.

5. Remove the paper from the back of the design.

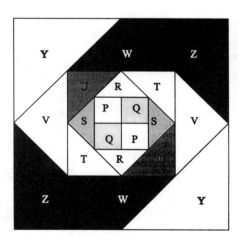

Quilt Top Assembly

1. Stitch the quilt top together into rows as diagramed below, and sew the rows together to form the quilt top. Press the seams between the blocks of each row in alternating directions to simplify the quilt top assembly.

2. Diagonally piece the first border, and cut lengths as needed. Attach side borders first and then the top and bottom border. Press all seams toward the border strips.

3. Trim final borders to fit and apply to the quilt top. Attach side borders first and then the top and bottom border strips. Press all seams toward the final border strips.

Snail's Trail

Fabric Requirements

	Lap Quilt 56" x 72" 35 8" blocks	Twin 72" x 96" 70 8" blocks	Double 80" x 96" 80 8" blocks
Background	2 1/2 yards	4 1/4 yards	4 3/4 yards
Dark Blues - Assorted	2 1/2 yards	4 1/4 yards	4 3/4 yards
Final Border	2 yards	2 3/4 yards	2 3/4 yards
Binding	5/8 yard	3/4 yard	3/4 yard
Backing	3 3/4 yards	5 3/4 yards	5 3/4 yards

Cutting Instructions

		Lap Quilt	Twin	Double	Special Directions
Background					
A	1 3/4" squares	70 (3 strips)	140 (6 strips)	160 (7 strips)	
B	2 3/4" squares	35 (3 strips)	70 (5 strips)	80 (6 strips)	cut once diagonally
C	3 1/4" squares	35 (3 strips)	70 (6 strips)	80 (7 strips)	cut once diagonally
D	4" squares	35 (4 strips)	70 (7 strips)	80 (8 strips)	cut once diagonally
E	5 1/4" squares	35 (5 strips)	70 (9 strips)	80 (10 strips)	cut once diagonally
Pieced Border					
	6 1/4" x 9 1/4" rectangles	8 (2 strips 6 1/2")	12 (3 strips 6 1/2")	12 (3 strips 6 1/2")	
Dark Blue - Assorted					
F	1 3/4" squares	70 (3 strips)	140 (6 strips)	160 (7 strips)	
G	2 3/4" squares	35 (3 strips)	70 (5 strips)	80 (6 strips)	cut once diagonally
H	3 1/4" squares	35 (3 strips)	70 (6 strips)	80 (7 strips)	cut once diagonally
I	4" squares	35 (4 strips)	70 (7 strips)	80 (8 strips)	cut once diagonally
J	5 1/4" squares	35 (5 strips)	70 (9 strips)	80 (10 strips)	cut once diagonally
Pieced Border					
	6 1/4" x 9 1/4" rectangles	8 (2 strips 6 1/2")	12 (3 strips 6 1/2")	12 (3 strips 6 1/2")	
Final Border - sides		2 - 6 1/2" x 64"	2 - 6 1/2" x 88"	2 - 6 1/2" x 88"	
		2 - 6 1/2" x 60"	2 - 6 1/2" x 76"	2 - 6 1/2" x 84"	
Binding - 2 1/2" strips		7 strips	9 strips	9 strips	

Snail's Trail Construction

1. Photocopy or trace the number of Snail's Trail foundations necessary for your chosen quilt. The foundation can be found on page 89.

Copy	Lap	35
	Twin	70
	Double	80

2. Stitch each **A** - 1 3/4" background square - to an **F** - a dark blue 1 3/4" square. Press each seam toward the darker fabric. Stitch each pair to another pair - alternating the darker square - to create "4-patch" blocks.

Make	Lap	35
	Twin	70
	Double	80

3. Paper piece the Snail's Trail blocks using the 4-patch unit from step 2 above as the center. Refer to the foundation paper **A/F** designation for the 4-patch placement. The sizes given in the cutting instructions are oversized for ease of assembly. Follow the paper piecing instructions given on pages 11 - 13 to create the blocks.

4. Trim the pieced units 1/4" past the outermost dotted line. This will leave a 1/4" seam allowance at the edge of the reel block. Each trimmed unit will measure 8 1/2" square

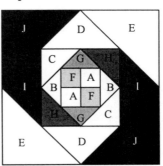

5. Remove the paper from the back of the design.

Pieced Border
Half Square Triangle Construction

NOTE The fabrics have been cut to allow for the use of triangle foundation papers when constructing half square triangles. If you wish to piece the triangles in the traditional method (triangle to triangle), cut each 6 1/4" x 9 1/4" rectangle into six 2 7/8" squares and cut each 2 7/8" square once diagonally. Each rectangle will produce twelve half square triangles 2 7/8".

1. Photocopy or trace the number of triangle foundation papers (found on page 86) necessary for your chosen quilt. The paper used will be three squares long x two squares wide.

Copy	Lap	8
	Twin	12
	Double	12

2. Place a 6 1/4" x 9 1/4" rectangle of background fabric right sides together with a 6 1/4" x 9 1/4" rectangle of dark blue fabric. Construct half square triangles following the triangle foundation paper method detailed on the paper. Each rectangle will yield twelve half square triangle units measuring 2 1/2".

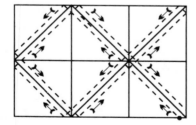

3. Stitch all half square triangles together into pairs as diagramed below. Press the seam as indicated by the arrow.

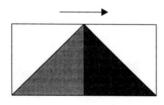

4. Join half square pairs together to create the border strips necessary for your chosen quilt. Press the seams as indicated by the arrows.

Sides - construct two border strips
- Lap - 14 triangle pairs (28 individual half squares)
- Twin - 20 triangle pairs
- Double - 20 triangle pairs

Top and Bottom - construct two border strips. To each end of the top and bottom border strips, add a 2 1/2" square of background fabric.
- Lap - 10 triangle pairs (20 individual half squares)
- Twin - 14 triangle pairs
- Double - 16 triangle pairs

Lap size borders diagramed

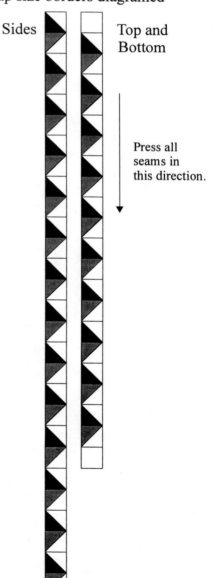

Sides

Top and Bottom

Press all seams in this direction.

Quilt Top Assembly

1. Stitch the blocks together into rows, and sew the rows together to form the quilt top:
lap - 5 x 7; twin - 7 x 10; and double - 8 x 10.

2. Add the pieced border strips. Attach the side bor-ders first and then the top and bottom border strips. Press the seams toward the pieced border.

4. Trim final borders to fit and apply to the quilt top. Attach side borders first and then the top and bottom borders. Press all seams toward the final border strips.

Hailey's Fan

Fabric Requirements

	Double 82" x 94" 30 10" blocks	**Queen** 94" x 106" 42 10" blocks
Background	3 1/4 yards	4 1/4 yards
Fan Blades	2 1/4 yards	3 yards
Fan Handles	1/2 yard	1 yard
Sashing and Posts	1 1/4 yards assorted prints 1 1/4 yards assorted solids	1 1/2 yards assorted prints 1 1/2 yards assorted solids
Final Border	2 3/4 yards	3 yards
Binding	3/4 yard	1 yard
Backing	7 1/2 yards	8 1/2 yards

Cutting Instructions

	Double	**Queen**
Background		
10 1/2" squares	30 (8 strips)	42 (11 strips)
2 1/2" strips - first border	7	9
Fan Blades		
6 1/4" wide strips	11	15
Fan Handle		
4" squares	30 (3 strips)	42 (5 strips)
Sashing and Posts		
1 1/2" strips - prints	21	29
1 1/2" strips - solids	21	29
Final Border - sides	2 - 8 1/2" x 82"	2 - 8 1/2" x 94"
- top and bottom	2 - 8 1/2" x 86"	2 - 8 1/2" x 98"
Binding		
2 1/2" strips	9	10

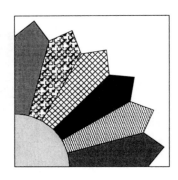

Block Construction

1. Trace and cut **Template D** and **E** from template plastic.

2. Layer the 6 1/4" wide strips of fan fabric right side up, raw edges even. Layer the fabric strips as deep as you can accurately cut — if you are comfortable cutting only two layers at once, layer only two strips.

3. Place **Template D** on the strip as diagramed. Trim off the waste at the left of the template, and then cut along the right edge of the template. Rotate the template and again cut along the right edge. Each strip should yield 17 Template D.

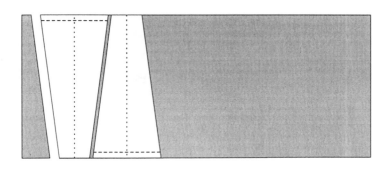

4. To trim the 4" squares of fan handle fabric, place **Template E** in one corner of each square and trace along the curved edge using a pencil. Cut along this curved line using scissors.

5. Fold each wedge (Template D) in half lengthwise, right sides together. Stitch across the top with a 1/4" seam, backstitch at each end of the seam. Chain stitch these pieces to speed production.

6. Snip the threads to separate the wedges. Clip the corner at the fold to eliminate bulk.

7. Gently finger press the short seam open, and then turn the point right side out. Line up the seam with the finger pressed crease. Press.

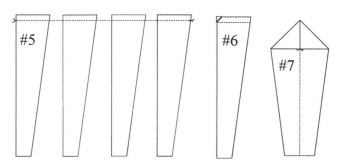

8. Arrange the wedges in the order that you would like them. Stitch wedges together in pairs using a 1/4" seam. Start the seam at the wide end on the wedge. It is most important that the wide end of the wedge is aligned. Backstitch at both ends of the seam. Stitch all wedges together into pairs. Press all seams open.

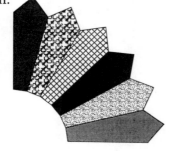

9. Stitch wedge pairs together to form the fan. Press all seams open.

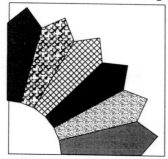

10. Place the pressed fans on to the 10 1/2" squares of background fabric. The two straight edges of the fan will align with the edges of the square. Baste the fan in place using tiny dots of basting glue.

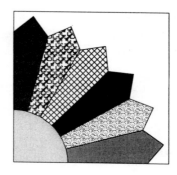

11. Cut quarter circles of freezer paper using **Template F**. Cut one for each fan handle.

12. Place **Template F** freezer paper on the wrong side of the fan handle fabric, with the shiny side of the freezer paper exposed.

13. Carefully roll the seam allowance over onto the freezer paper template using the tip of a warm iron. The seam allowance will lightly adhere to the freezer paper.

14. Place the fan handle in place on the fan/background fabric assembly. Baste the fan handle in place using tiny dots of basting glue.

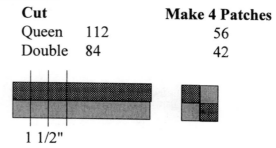

15. Applique the fan and the fan handle to the background fabric using a machine applique stitch. I use a stitch that is a loose zig-zag. The length is set at 2 and the width at .5 or .75. Practice with the stitch to find the stitch you are most comfortable with.

Sashing and Post Construction

1. Stitch each 1 1/2" wide strip of print fabric to a 1 1/2" wide strip of solid fabric. Press the seam toward the solid fabric.

2. Cut the sewn strips into 10 1/2" lengths.

Cut	Queen	97
	Double	71

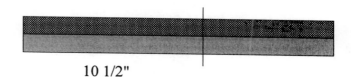

10 1/2"

3. Cut the remaining strips and strip segments into units 1 1/2" wide. Stitch units together to create 4 patch units.

Cut		Make 4 Patches
Queen	112	56
Double	84	42

1 1/2"

Quilt Top Assembly

1. Stitch the blocks together into rows, and sew the rows together to form the quilt top:
double - 5 x 6, and queen - 6 x 7. Place sashing strips between blocks and at the row ends as diagramed.   Stitch and press the seams toward the sashing strips.

2. Diagonally piece the first border, and cut lengths as needed. Attach side borders first and then the top and bottom borders. Press the seams toward the border strips.

3. Add the pieced border strips. Attach the side borders first and then the top and bottom border strips. Press the seams toward the first border.

4. Trim final borders to fit and apply to the quilt top. Attach side borders first and then the top and bottom borders. Press all seams toward the final border strips.

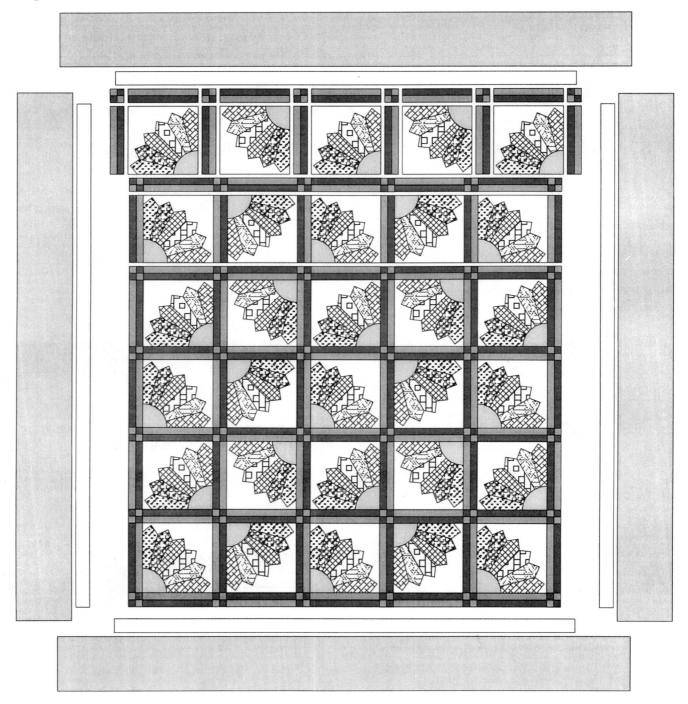

Puzzling Hexes

Fabric Requirements

	Twin	**Queen**
	71" x 98"	92" x 98"
	33 stars	46 stars
Background	3 1/2 yards	4 1/2 yards
Dark Fabrics - assorted	1 3/4 yards	2 1/4 yards
Light Fabrics - assorted	1 3/4 yards	2 1/4 yards
First Border	1/2 yard	1/2 yard
Final Border	3 yards	3 yards
Binding	3/4 yard	1 yard
Backing	6 yards	8 1/2 yards

Cutting Instructions

	Twin	Queen
Background	13 strips 6 1/2" wide 3 strips 3 1/2" wide 2 strips 2 1/4" wide 4 strips 2 1/2" wide	18 strips 6 1/2" wide 4 strips 3 1/2" wide 2 strips 2 1/4" wide 4 strips 2 1/2" wide
Dark Fabrics	13 strips 4" wide	18 strips 4" wide
Light Fabrics	13 strips 4" wide	18 strips 4" wide
First Border	8 strips 1 1/2" wide	9 strips 1 1/2" wide
Final Border - sides	2 - 6 1/2" x 96 1/2" 2 - 6 1/2" x 76"	2 - 6 1/2" x 96 1/2" 2 - 6 1/2" x 96 1/2"
Binding	9 strips 2 1/2"	10 strips 2 1/2"

Strip Subcutting

1. To subcut the light and dark fabric strips, place the 4 1/4" line of the 60° Clear View Triangle Ruler at the lower raw edge of your 4" wide strip. **YES**, the tip of your ruler will fall off the top edge of the strip! Trim off the waste at the left edge of the ruler, and then cut along the right edge of the ruler. Rotate the ruler and again cut along the right edges. You may cut the strip using **Template G** if the 60° Clear View ruler is not available in your area. **Cut 8 triangles 4 1/4" (Template G) from each strip.**

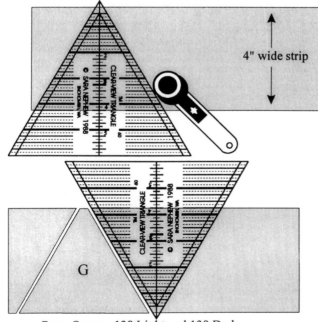

Cut: Queen   138 Light and 138 Dark
       Twin   99 Light and 99 Dark

2. Trim the remaining portion of the 4" strips to 3 3/4" wide. Subcut the trimmed strip using the **60° Clear View Triangle Ruler** as diagramed at the left. This time placing the 3 3/4" marking of the ruler along the lower raw edge of the strip. **Cut 8 triangles 3 3/4" (Template H) from each strip.**

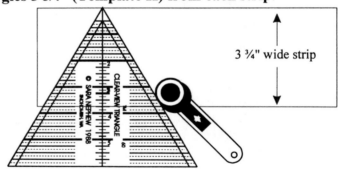

Cut: Queen   138 Light and 138 Dark
       Twin   99 Light and 99 Dark

3. Cut the 6 1/2" wide strips of background fabric into hexagons using **Template I** as your guide. Each strip should yield 5 hexagons.

Cut: Queen   90 Template I
       Twin   64 Template I

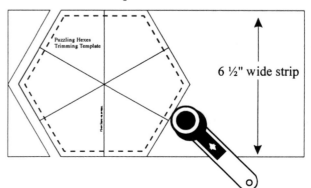

4. Cut the background 3 1/2" strips to size as diagramed below. The cut units will become portions of the top and bottom row when piecing the quilt top.

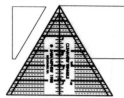

3 ½" wide strip
background fabric

Trim the left edge using the 60° Clear View Triangle Ruler.

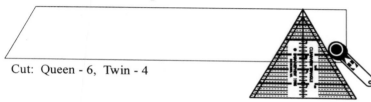

— 21 3/8" —

Measure 21 3/8" from the point and mark a dot at the edge of the fabric strip.

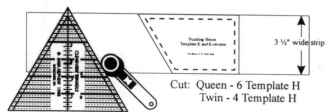

Cut: Queen - 6, Twin - 4

Line up the 60° Clear View Triangle Ruler at the dot and cut a 60° angle in the direction opposite the original cut. **Cut: Queen 6**
Twin 4

5. Cut **Template H, Template K and Template K reverse** from the remaining 3 1/2" strip of background fabric. Fold the strip in half to produce Template K and K-reverse at the same time. Place the 3 3/4" marking of the ruler along the lower edge of the strip. The tip of the ruler will fall off the edge of the strip.

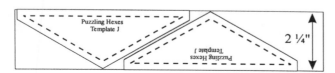

Puzzling Hexes
Template K and K-reverse

3 ½" wide strip

Cut: Queen - 6 Template H
Twin - 4 Template H

6. Cut the 2 1/4" strips of background fabric using **Template J** as diagramed below. You will need 14 template E for either the twin or queen size quilt.

Puzzling Hexes
Template J

Puzzling Hexes
Template J

2 ¼"

Block Construction

1. Stitch a dark triangle G to a light triangle G (4 1/4" triangles). Place the dark triangle on top for 46 pairs. Place the light triangle on top for a second set of 46 pairs. Stitch from the wide end to the point. Press the seams in one direction.

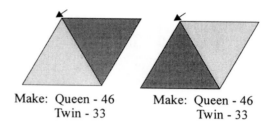

Make: Queen - 46
Twin - 33

Make: Queen - 46
Twin - 33

2. Add a third triangle to each triangle pair to create half hex units. Press the seams in one direction.

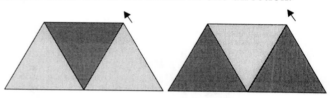

Make: Queen - 46 of each unit
Twin - 33 of each unit

3. Stitch half hex units together to complete the hexagons.

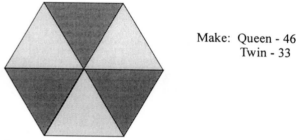

Make: Queen - 46
Twin - 33

4. Trim each completed hexagon using the Trimming Template I. Be sure to place the diagonal lines on the sewn seam lines.

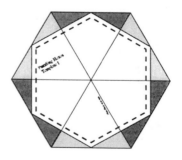

Quilt Top Assembly - Twin Diagram

1. Arrange the pieced hexagons, light and dark **H** triangles, and assorted background pieces together as shown in the diagram below. Note the placement of the **H** triangles in relation to the pieced hexagons. This placement creates the spinning effect of the star.

2. Stitch the units together into rows. The **H** triangles are sewn to hexagons to create diamond shaped units that will be sewn together to form the rows. Press all seams toward the **H** triangles.

3. Diagonally piece the 2 1/2" wide background strips together. Cut to length as needed and apply to each side of the quilt top. Press the seams toward the background strip.

4. Diagonally piece the first border strips together, cut lengths as needed and apply to the quilt. Attach side borders first and then the top and bottom borders. Press all seams toward the border strips.

5. Trim final borders to fit and apply to the quilt top. Attach side borders first and then the top and bottom borders. Press all seams toward the final border strips.

Twin Size Quilt Assembly Diagram

Quilt Top Assembly - Queen Diagram

1. Arrange the pieced hexagons, light and dark **H** triangles, and assorted background pieces together as shown in the diagram below. Note the placement of the **H** triangles in relation to the pieced hexagons. This placement creates the spinning effect of the star.

2. Stitch the units together into rows. The **H** triangles are sewn to hexagons to create diamond shaped units that will be sewn together to form the rows. Press all seams toward the **H** triangles.

3. Diagonally piece the 2 1/2" wide background strips together. Cut to length as needed and apply to each side of the quilt top. Press the seams toward the background strip.

4. Diagonally piece the first border strips together, cut lengths as needed and apply to the quilt. Attach side borders first and then the top and bottom borders. Press all seams toward the border strips.

5. Trim final borders to fit and apply to the quilt top. Attach side borders first and then the top and bottom borders. Press all seams toward the final border strips.

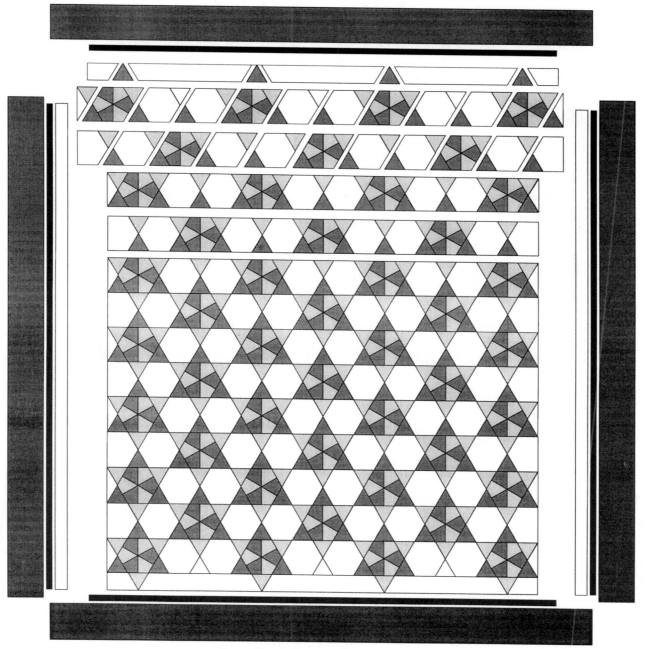

Queen Size Quilt Assembly Diagram

Scrap Hunter

Fabric Requirements

	Lap Quilt 50" x 68" 24 9" blocks	**Twin** 68" x 86" 48 9" blocks	**Queen** 86" x 104" 80 9" blocks
Background - Assorted	1 3/4 yards	2 1/2 yards	4 yards
Dark Blues - Assorted	1 3/4 yards	2 1/2 yards	4 yards
First Border	1/2 yard	1/2 yard	5/8 yard
Final Border	1 3/4 yards	2 3/8 yards	3 yards
Binding	5/8 yard	3/4 yard	1 yard
Backing	3 1/4 yards	5 1/4 yards	7 3/4 yards

Cutting Instructions

	Lap Quilt	Twin	Queen	Special Directions
Background				
A 7 1/4" squares	12 (3 strips)	24 (5 strips)	40 (8 strips)	cut once diagonally
L 2 3/8" strips	24 (4 strips)	48 (8 strips)	80 (14 strips)	cut strips using template L
M 2 3/8" strips	48 (5 strips)	96 (9 strips)	160 (15 strips)	cut strips using template M
Dark Blues - Assorted				
A 7 1/4" squares	12 (3 strips)	24 (5 strips)	40 (8 strips)	cut once diagonally
L 2 3/8" strips	24 (4 strips)	48 (8 strips)	80 (14 strips)	cut strips using template L
M 2 3/8" strips	48 (5 strips)	96 (9 strips)	160 (15 strips)	cut strips using template M
First Border				
1 1/2" strips	5 strips	7 strips	9 strips	
Final Border - sides	2 - 6 1/2" x 60"	2 - 6 1/2" x 78"	2 - 6 1/2" x 96"	
	2 - 6 1/2" x 54"	2 - 6 1/2" x 72"	2 - 6 1/2" x 90"	
Binding - 2 1/2" strips	6 strips	8 strips	10 strips	

Sub Cutting

1. Squares - cut each 7 1/4" square once diagonally.

2. Trapezoids - layer several **L** strips. Layer the fabric only as deep as you can accurately cut.

3. Place **Template L** at the end of the strips. Butt a ruler up to the diagonal edge of the template, remove the template, and cut along the edge of the ruler. Be sure to cut through all layers. Place the template back on to the strip, using a ruler, cut along the opposite end of Template L, creating trapezoids.

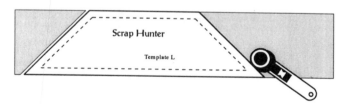

4. Rotate the template and place it onto the layered strip again. Butt the edge of a ruler against the edge of the template, remove the template and cut along the edge of the ruler. Continue this cutting method along the full length of the **L** fabric strips.

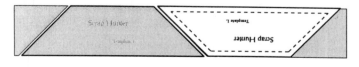

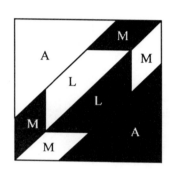

5. Diamonds - Layer several **M** strips. **Template M** must be cut from folded strips. Trim off the selvages at the end of the strip. Place **Template M** at the trimmed end of the strips. Cut along the diagonal edge. Continue cutting **Template M** along the full length of the **M** fabric strips.

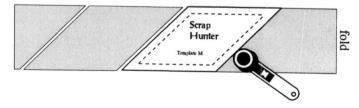

6. Cutting Template M from a folded strip will create a right and left diamond with each cut.

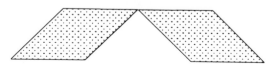

Block Construction

1. Stitch a diamond to both ends of each trapezoid. Each dark blue trapezoid will receive 2 light diamonds, and each light blue trapezoid will receive 2 dark diamonds. Place the fabric grain on each diamond as indicated by the "stripes" shown below. This will place the grain of the fabric along the outer edge of each block and give the most stable results.

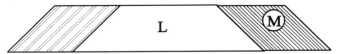

2. Begin and end the seam at the "1/4" notch" as diagramed below. This will produce a straight edge along the sewn strip.

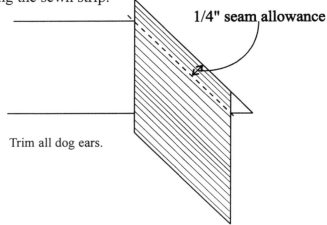

1/4" seam allowance

Trim all dog ears.

3. Press all seams toward the darker fabric, whether that be the trapezoid or diamonds.

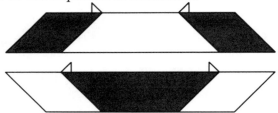

4. To each trapezoid unit stitch a half square triangle. The triangle should be the same "color" as the trapezoid - light blue trapezoid/light blue triangle. Press the seam toward the dark diamonds, or toward the dark triangle. Refer to the diagram below.

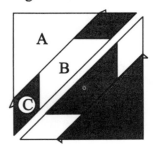

5. Stitch the half block units together at the center seam. The seams at the diamonds will be opposing seams and stitch together easily. Press the center seam toward the dark blue trapezoid. All of the long seams of the block will be pressed in one direction. This will cause the seams to be opposing if the quilt is assembled as diagramed on page 76.

Quilt Top Assembly

1. Stitch the blocks together into rows, and sew the rows together to form the quilt top: lap - 4x6; twin - 6x8; and queen - 8 x 10. Press the seams between the blocks of each row in alternating directions to simplify the quilt top assembly.

2. Diagonally piece the first border, and cut lengths as needed. Attach side borders first and then the top and bottom border. Press all seams toward the border strips.

3. Trim final borders to fit and apply to the quilt top. Attach side borders first and then the top and bottom border strips. Press all seams toward the final border strips.

Optional Quilt Top Assembly

When assembled as diagramed below, the seams will no longer oppose one another. You may choose to re-press the 3 long seams in some of the blocks to facilitate the quilt top construction.

If you choose to increase the size of this quilt, enlarge the quilt in increments of 2, 6 x 6 blocks, 6 x 8 blocks, etc. This will allow the same pattern to repeat at all of the corners.

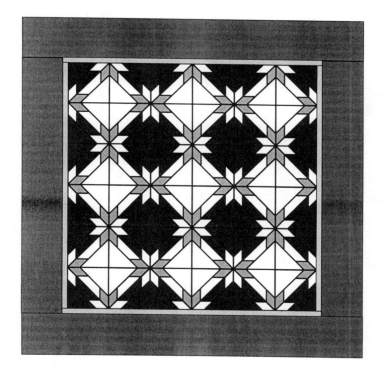

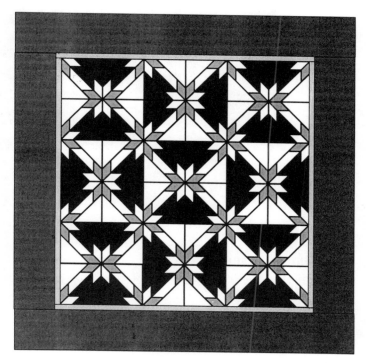

Drunkard's Path

Fabric Requirements

	Lap 64" x 80"	Queen 88" x 104"
Light Blues - Assorted	3 1/4 yards	5 1/2 yards
Dark Blues - Assorted	4 1/2 yards	7 1/2 yards
Binding	3/4 yard	1 yard
Backing	4 yards	8 yards

Cutting Instructions

	Lap	Queen	Special Instructions
Light Blues - Assorted			
O 4 1/2" squares	100 squares (12 strips)	196 squares (22 strips)	trim with Template O
N 3 1/4" squares	152 squares (13 strips)	284 squares (24 strips)	trim with Template N
Dark Blues - Assorted			
O 4 1/2" squares	152 squares (17 strips)	284 squares (32 strips)	trim with Template O
4 1/2" squares	68 squares (8 strips)	92 squares (10 strips)	
N 3 1/4" squares	100 squares (9 strips)	196 squares (17 strips)	trim with Template N
Binding			
2 1/2" strips	7 strips	10 strips	
Final Border - sides	2 - 6 1/2" x 79"	2 - 6 1/2" x 100"	
- top and bottom	2 - 6 1/2" x 90"	2 - 6 1/2" x 90"	

1. Trim 4 1/2" squares using **Template O**.

Trim	Lap	152 - dark blue
		100 - light blue
	Queen	284 - dark blue
		196 - light blue

The remaining 4 1/2" squares of dark blue fabric (Lap - 68 and Queen - 92) will be reserved for block construction.

Template O
Drunkard's Path

2. Trim all 3 1/4" squares using **Template N**.

Template N
Drunkard's Path

Unit Construction

1. Fold each **N** and **O** in half and lightly finger crease the fabric edge to mark the center point on each curved edge.

2. Place **N** and **O** (one light blue piece and one dark blue piece) right sides together, match center mark

and pin. Line up straight edges and pin at either end.

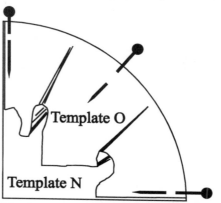

Template O

Template N

3. Stitch with the concave edge (**Template O**) on top. Using a stiletto to coax the concave edge into alignment, stitch with a 1/4" seam. Do not stitch more than 1/2" to 1" at a time before you re-align the edges.

4. Press the seam toward the darker fabric.

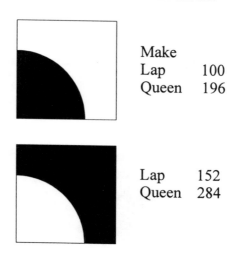

Make
Lap   100
Queen   196

Lap   152
Queen   284

Block Construction

1. Arrange units constructed in the previous step into the pattern diagramed below. Press the seams as indicated by the arrows.

Make Lap   4 complete blocks
          Queen 6 complete blocks

2. Arrange units from previous page into the pattern diagramed below. These units will be placed at the top and bottom of the quilt to complete the pattern.

Make Lap   4 top and bottom border units
          Queen 6 top and bottom border units

3. Arrange units from previous page into the pattern diagramed below. These units will be placed at the sides of the quilt to complete the pattern.

Make Lap   4 side border units
          Queen 6 side border units

4. Arrange units from previous page into the pattern diagramed below. These units will be placed at the corners of the quilt to complete the pattern.

Make Lap   2 left and 2 right corner units
          Queen 2 left and 2 right corner units

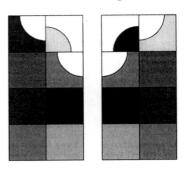

Quilt Top Assembly - Lap Size Diagram

1. Arrange the blocks and partial blocks on the floor or a design wall, follow the diagram below to help you order the blocks in the proper arrangement.

2. Stitch the blocks and partial blocks into rows. Sew the rows together to form the quilt top.

Quilt Top Assembly - Queen Size Diagram

1. Arrange the blocks and partial blocks on the floor or a design wall, Follow the diagram below to help you order the blocks in the proper arrangement.

2. Stitch the blocks and partial blocks into rows. Sew the rows together to form the quilt top.

Finishing

Borders

All of the quilts in this book were constructed using square borders. The application of a square border is easier to master than the application of a mitered border.

Primary Borders

Primary borders are all border strips that are attached to the quilt top before the final border. They may be very narrow, wide, piped, or even pieced. All primary borders for the quilts in this text were cut as crossgrain strips and pieced together using diagonal seaming. Diagonal seams in the border strips are less visible than straight seams; no effort is made to place the seams in any particular position.

To make a diagonal seam, place the first strip right side up. Position the second fabric strip right side down on top of the first strip. The second strip will be placed at a right angle to the first. Stitch diagonally across the strip ends. Trim the excess to 1/4" and press the seam to one side. All of the "First (Second or Third) Border" strips are sewn together to create a long strip, and the necessary lengths are cut from it.

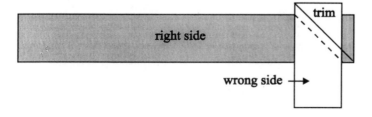

Pieced Borders

A pieced border is generally one of the primary borders. It is a wonderful addition to a beautiful quilt. A pieced border must be mathematically correct to fit the quilt top. If your piecing has been less that accurate, it is possible to adjust the vertical seams of the border strip to accommodate the difference. Unfortunately, this will also adjust where the points of the pieced border fall.

Piped Border

Piped borders are especially fun in places that you would like a little "hit" of color. The piped border strips are pieced diagonally to create a long strip. Trim the excess fabric to 1/4" seam allowance and press these seams open. Press the 1" wide strip in half lengthwise - wrong sides together. This will result in a 1/2" wide strip.

The piped border strips are cut to length and basted to the edge of the quilt top, raw edges even. The strips will remain in this position, with the fold toward the center of the quilt. After the next border is applied, the piped border will measure 1/4" wide.

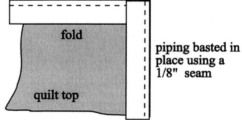

Final Border

The final border is cut from the lengthwise grain of the fabric. This will require extra yardage to be purchased, but it is well worth the expense.

The lengthwise grain of the fabric is more stable than the crossgrain. This extra stability will go a long way toward preventing stretching and ruffling of the quilt edge due to handling.

To cut a lengthwise fabric strip, measure the inches of fabric called for in the directions, and cut the yardage to that length. Fold the fabric crosswise, until it is narrow enough to be spanned by your rotary ruler. The folded fabric will have selvage at either edge. The first cut will be to remove the selvage. Cut the border strips to size. Use the rulings on the cutting mat if your ruler is too narrow.

Applying Borders

The individual quilt instructions in this book do not give exact measurements for the borders. The strip measurements given are longer than what would be mathematically correct. No matter how carefully you have pieced, over the course of **many** seams, variations do occur. It is not uncommon for the sides of a quilt top to have stretched with the handling that they have received, or even measure differently. These variations need to be addressed if you wish to have a square quilt that lays flat.

To accommodate the variations, do not cut a strip to the length that is mathematically correct, and do not stitch a long length to the side of the quilt top and cut off where the edge of the quilt lands!!!

Measuring

When adding borders it is important to measure the "body" of the quilt top, not the edges of the quilt where stretching may have occurred.

1. Press the quilt top carefully. When measuring, it is important that the quilt lay as flat and smooth as possible.

2. Measure from top to bottom through the center of the quilt with a metal measuring tape. My sewing bag contains a petite 10 foot tape measure. Cut the two side borders to that measurement.

3. Pin the border strips in place along the sides of the quilt top. Match the center of the border strip to the center of the quilt top. Use as many pins as necessary.

4. Stitch the border strip to the quilt top. You are making the quilt top fit the border strip! Stitch with the border strip on top. The feed dogs will help to ease in the fullness of the quilt top if necessary.

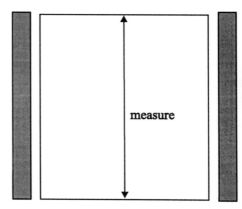

cut 2 border strips to the measured length

measure

5. From the right side, press the seams toward the border strips.

6. Lay the quilt on a flat surface and measure the quilt top from side to side through the center of the quilt, including the border pieces that you just added. Cut the top and bottom border strips to that measurement.

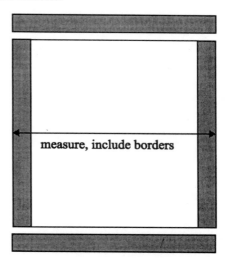

measure, include borders

7. Pin and stitch these borders in the same manner that the side borders were added.

8. Press the seams toward the border strip.

All borders will be added in this manner. When applying the final border, backtack the seams that will be exposed at the raw edge of the quilt. This helps to prevent the stitches from pulling out as the quilt top is layered and quilted. The quilts in this book have had the side borders applied first, and then the top and bottom borders. This order of border application is generally a more economical use of fabric - a shorter yardage of fabric is required.

Backing

How to prepare the backing is a matter of personal taste. Many quilters use the leftover scraps of the quilt top to piece together a scrappy backing. If you are planning to hand quilt the layers, a pieced backing may not be the best idea. The many seams might be difficult to "needle". Fortunately, fabric manufacturers are thinking about backings, and have made available fabric that is 100" - 112" wide. This fabric is very easy to use; simply cut to size. There are no seams to make the quilting process difficult.

Select a backing fabric that is a good quality cotton. Do not purchase a poor quality piece of fabric because it is less expensive. The backing needs to wear as well as the quilt top. A bed sheet really is not an ideal quilt backing. The fabric of a bed sheet is very tightly woven, and may make hand quilting a chore, perhaps even a painful experience.

The effect of the backing fabric color needs to be considered. If a polyester batting is used, a dark backing fabric may show through, dulling the light or bright colors of the quilt top. If the backing is patterned, the quilt top may appear splotchy! Cotton batting is more opaque and will allow less shadowing.

Yardage Requirements

Backing should be 6" - 8" larger than the completed quilt top. Yardage is figured on 43" of usable fabric width after preshrinking and removing the selvages. Measure the quilt top to determine the length and width.

- widths up to 37"   length + 6"

- widths 38" to 80"   (length x 2) + 12"
    Remove the selvages and sew one
    lengthwise seam. Press to one side.

- widths greater than 80" (width x 3) + 18"
    Remove the selvages and sew two
    crosswise seams. Press to one side

Press the seam open if you plan to hand quilt.

Batting

Batting is the layer of filling between the quilt top and the backing. There are many weights and types of batting available on the market today. It is available in polyester, cotton, cotton/polyester blends and even wool. Batting is available packaged in standard sizes or as yardage from a bolt. Some are better suited to hand quilting while others are best left for tying.

Bonded Polyester

Polyester has been widely used as batting for many years. It has been in just the last few years that cotton and cotton /polyester blends have started to reclaim the market. Polyester batts are available in different weights and thicknesses. The thinner polyester batts mimic the look of a cotton batt, and are easy to hand quilt. The thicker batts are difficult to hand quilt and are used for hand tied quilts.

Polyester fibers tend to migrate. Once the fibers reach the surface of the quilt top, they ball together. This migration is called bearding. Polyester batting is especially guilty of this problem and it is particularly visible on dark quilts. A grey polyester batting is available for use in dark quilts, making the bearding less noticeable.

100% Cotton or Cotton/Polyester Blends

The cotton battings will give a more traditional look to your quilts. 100% cotton batting generally requires more quilting than a polyester batting would, but batting manufacturers are constantly upgrading and improving their product. The traditional cotton batting needs to be quilted every 1/4" - 1/2" to prevent the fibers from clumping. Cotton batting is available today that can be quilted 8" apart!

Cotton/polyester batting is my personal favorite. I prefer the antique look that the cotton batting gives. Cotton/ polyester batting hand quilts nicely and is a great choice for machine quilting. As you select and purchase batting, my best advice is to read the package!! Know what you are working with to prevent disappointment.

Quilting

Quilting is the process by which the three layers of the quilt (top, batting and backing) are held together. Quilting can be accomplished by hand or by machine. And, if you have no inclination to quilt, the three layers can be held together by tying. Entire books are available on the subject of quilting, both hand and machine. I will refer you to your local quilt shop. They can help you find the text that you need.

Binding

Binding is the process of finishing the edge of the quilt after it is quilted.

Preparation

•Baste the edge of the quilt top down. This can be done with a long, wide zig-zag stitch on the sewing machine. This basting will prevent excess shifting of the quilt top layer at the edge as the binding is applied.

•Trim the batting and backing 1/8" beyond the raw edge of the quilt top. This extra fabric and batting will fill out the binding and prevent empty spaces.

•Piece the cut binding strips together using a diagonal seam. Trim the seams to 1/4" and press the seams open.

•Press the long binding strip in half lengthwise, right side out, to a width of 1 1/4".

Attach the Binding

•Position the binding strips so that its lengthwise raw edges are even with the raw edge of the quilt top. Start stitching 1/4" from the corner of the quilt top, backtack to secure the seam and stitch to the opposite end. Stop stitching 1/4" from the quilt corner and backtack.

•Remove the quilt from the sewing machine, and snip threads. Rotate the quilt to prepare to sew the next edge.

•Fold the binding strip up, away from the quilt, it will fold nicely at a 45° angle. Fold it again to bring the strip edge along the raw edge of the quilt top, leaving a 2" - 3" tail of binding extending beyond

the corner. Lower the needle into the binding at the point where the first seam stopped, 1/4" from the corner of the quilt top, backtack and stitch to the opposite corner of the quilt top.

•Continue around the quilt in this manner until you reach the corner where you began stitching. Fold the first section binding strip out of the way as you stitch to the end of the final binding length. Stitch to 1/4" from the corner and backtack.

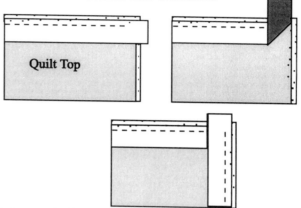

Mitered Corners

•To finish the corners of the binding, fold the tail of the binding so that it lays flat. Draw a line perpendicular to the seam line, starting at the end of the seam, **A**. Draw a second line at a 45° from the first line, **B**. Draw a third line, **C**, at a 45° from the opposite end of line **A**. The intersection of lines **B** and **C** will be a 90° angle.

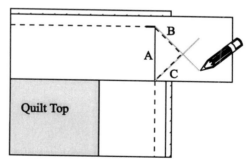

•With a small stitch, sew directly on lines **B** and **C**, pivot at the point, and backtack at each end of the seam. Trim to a 1/4" seam allowance. Turn the stitched corner right side out.

•Roll the binding over the raw edge of the quilt. Hand stitch the fold of the binding to the stitching line on the backside of the quilt.

Triangle Foundation Paper Master

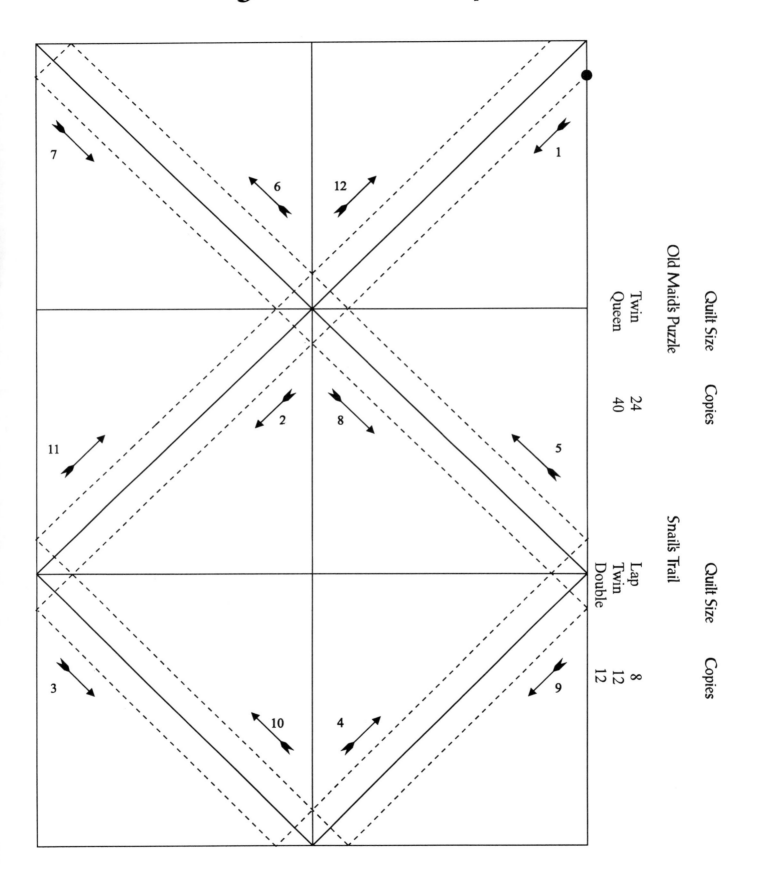

Quilt Size	Copies		Quilt Size	Copies
Old Maid's Puzzle			**Snail's Trail**	
Twin	24		Lap	8
Queen	40		Twin	12
			Double	12

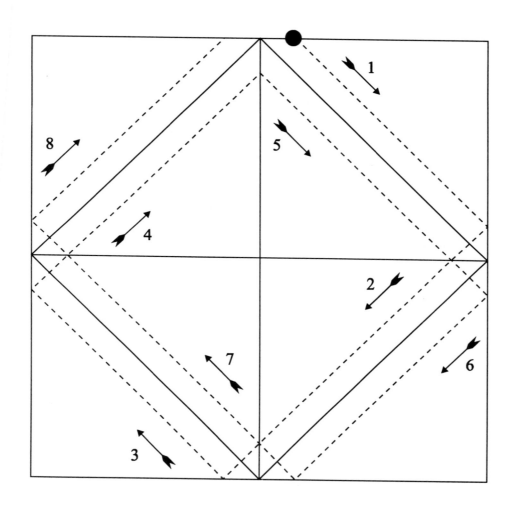

Triangle Foundation Paper

Quilt Size	Copies
Flannel Star	
Wall Hanging	54
Double	72

Whirlpool Foundation Master

Photocopy or trace 33 copies.

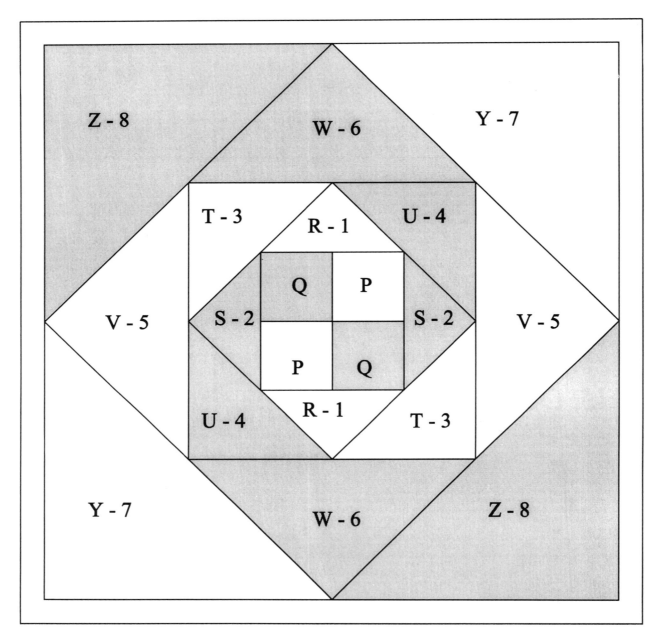

Trim sewn block on the outermost line to give a ¼" seam allowance. The letter designation indicates fabric piece used. The number designation indicates the piecing sequence.

Snail's Trail Foundation Master

Photocopy or trace: Lap - 35, Twin - 70, and Double - 80.

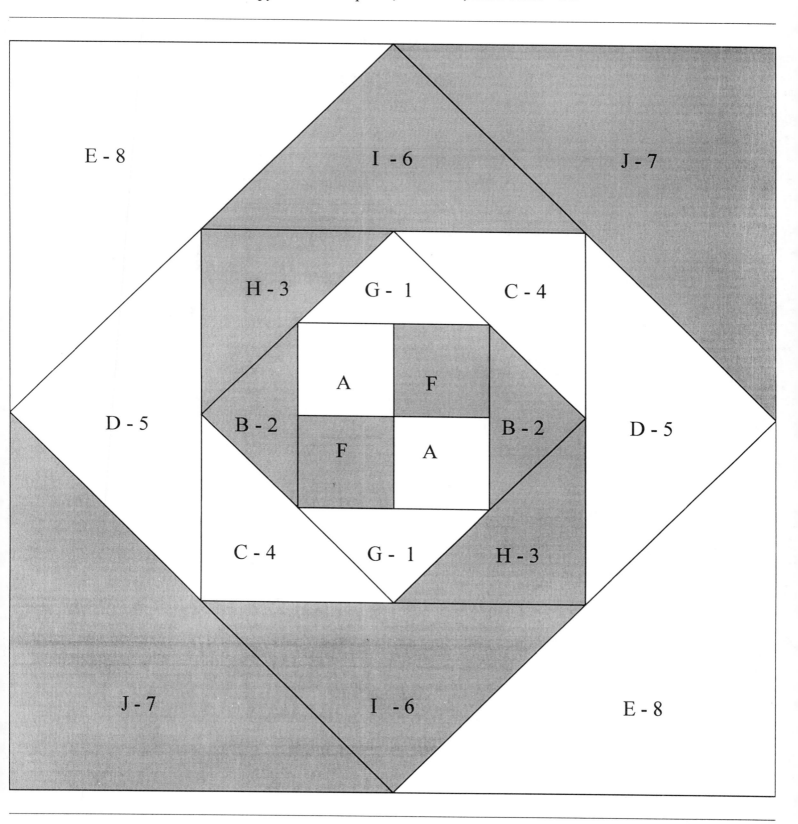

Add 1/4" when trimming completed block to give a 1/4" seam allowance.
The letter designation indicates fabric piece used. The number designation
indicates the piecing sequence.

Templates

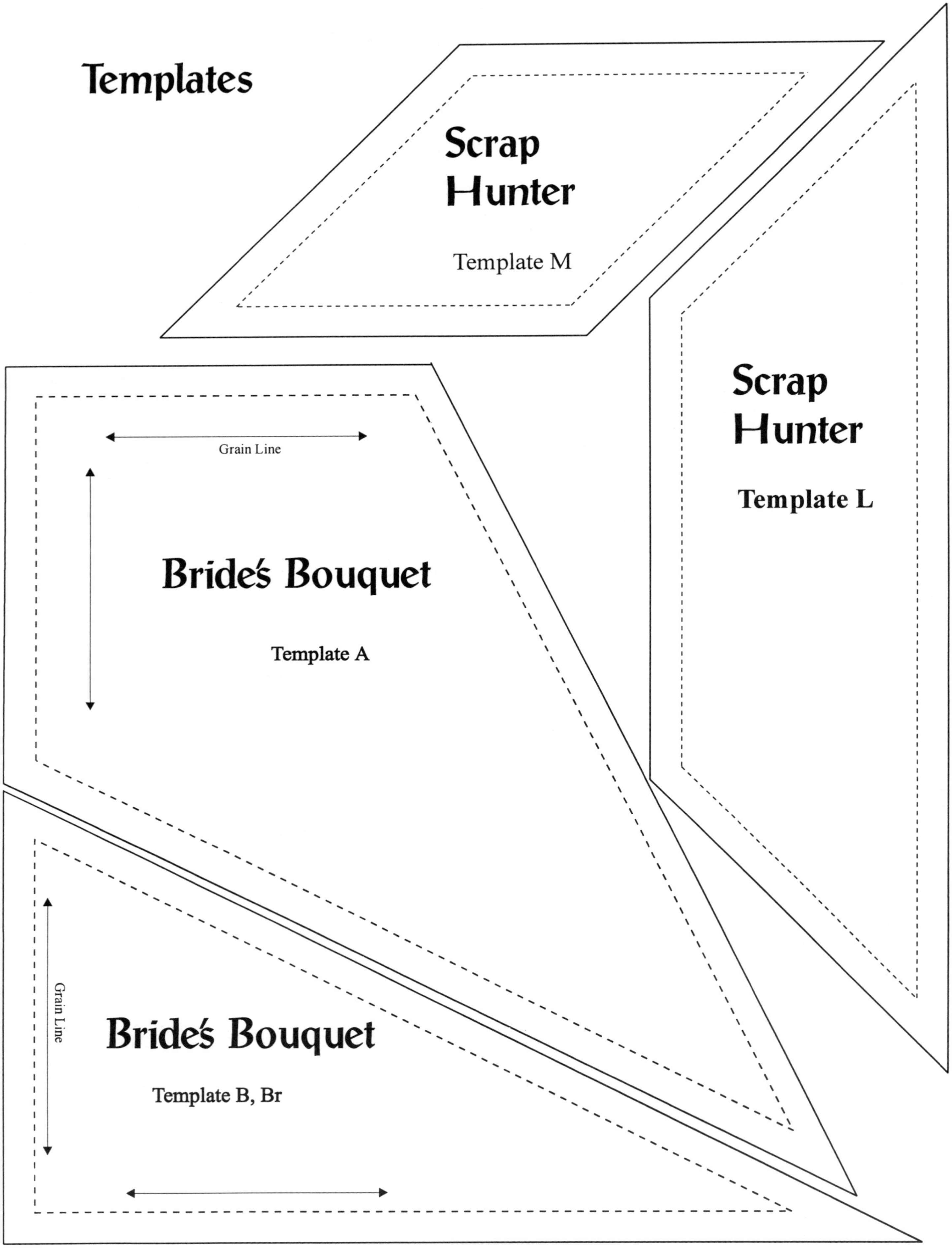

Scrap Hunter

Template M

Scrap Hunter

Template L

Grain Line

Bride's Bouquet

Template A

Grain Line

Bride's Bouquet

Template B, Br

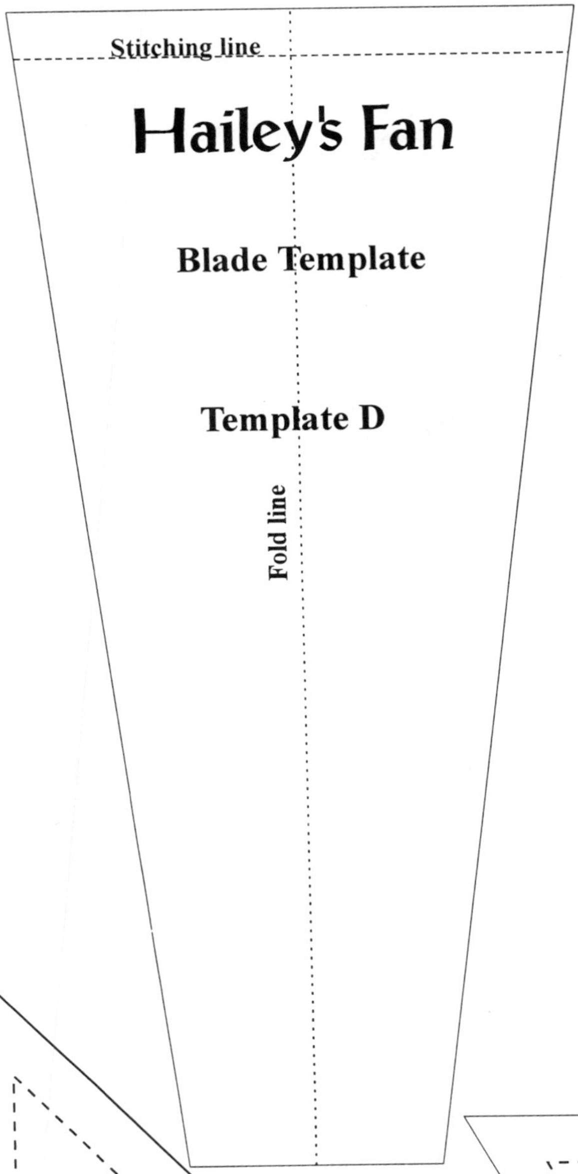

Stitching line

Hailey's Fan

Blade Template

Template D

Fold line

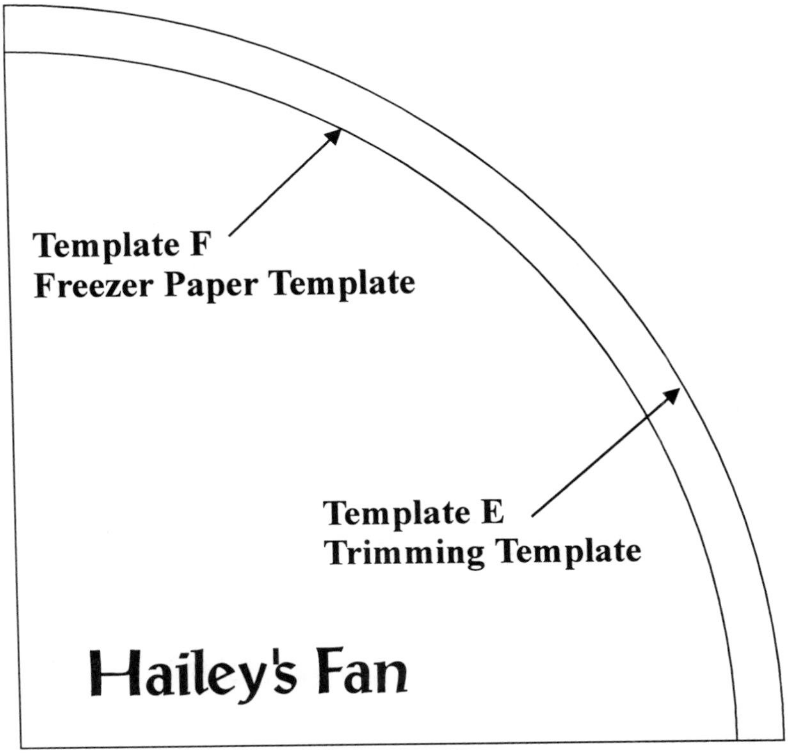

Template F
Freezer Paper Template

Template E
Trimming Template

Hailey's Fan

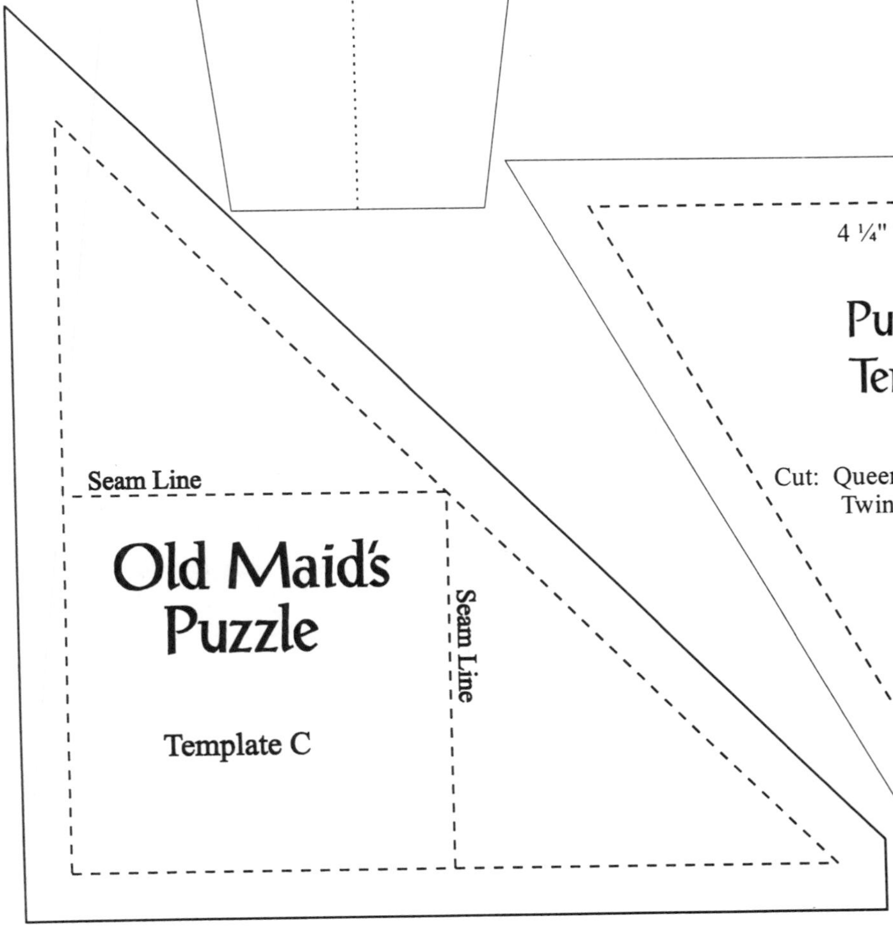

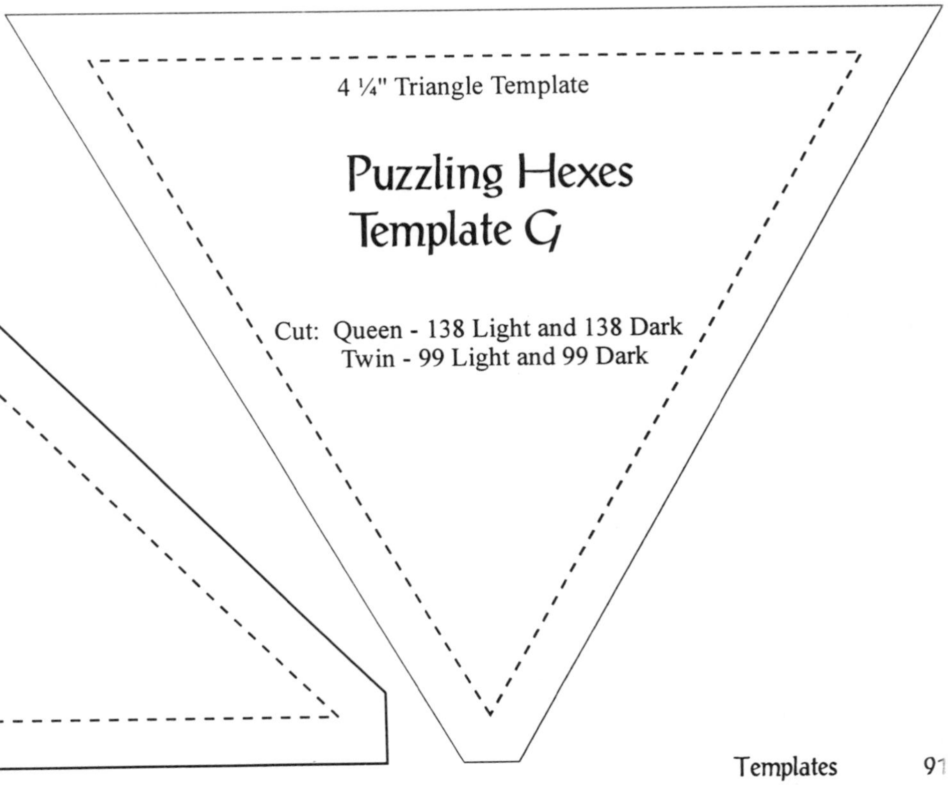

4 ¼" Triangle Template

Puzzling Hexes
Template G

Cut: Queen - 138 Light and 138 Dark
Twin - 99 Light and 99 Dark

Seam Line

Old Maid's
Puzzle

Seam Line

Template C

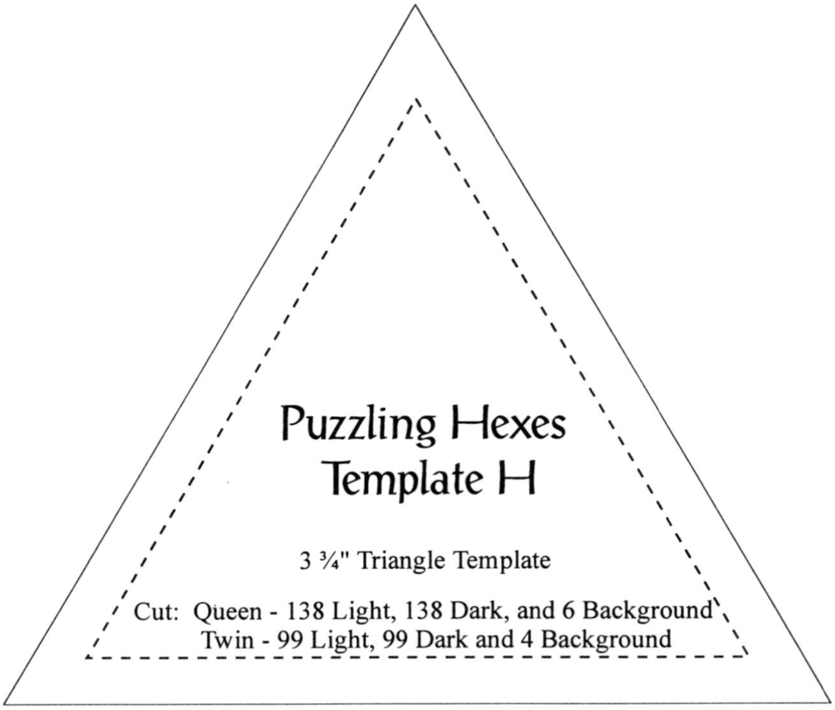

Puzzling Hexes
Template H

3 ¾" Triangle Template

Cut: Queen - 138 Light, 138 Dark, and 6 Background
Twin - 99 Light, 99 Dark and 4 Background

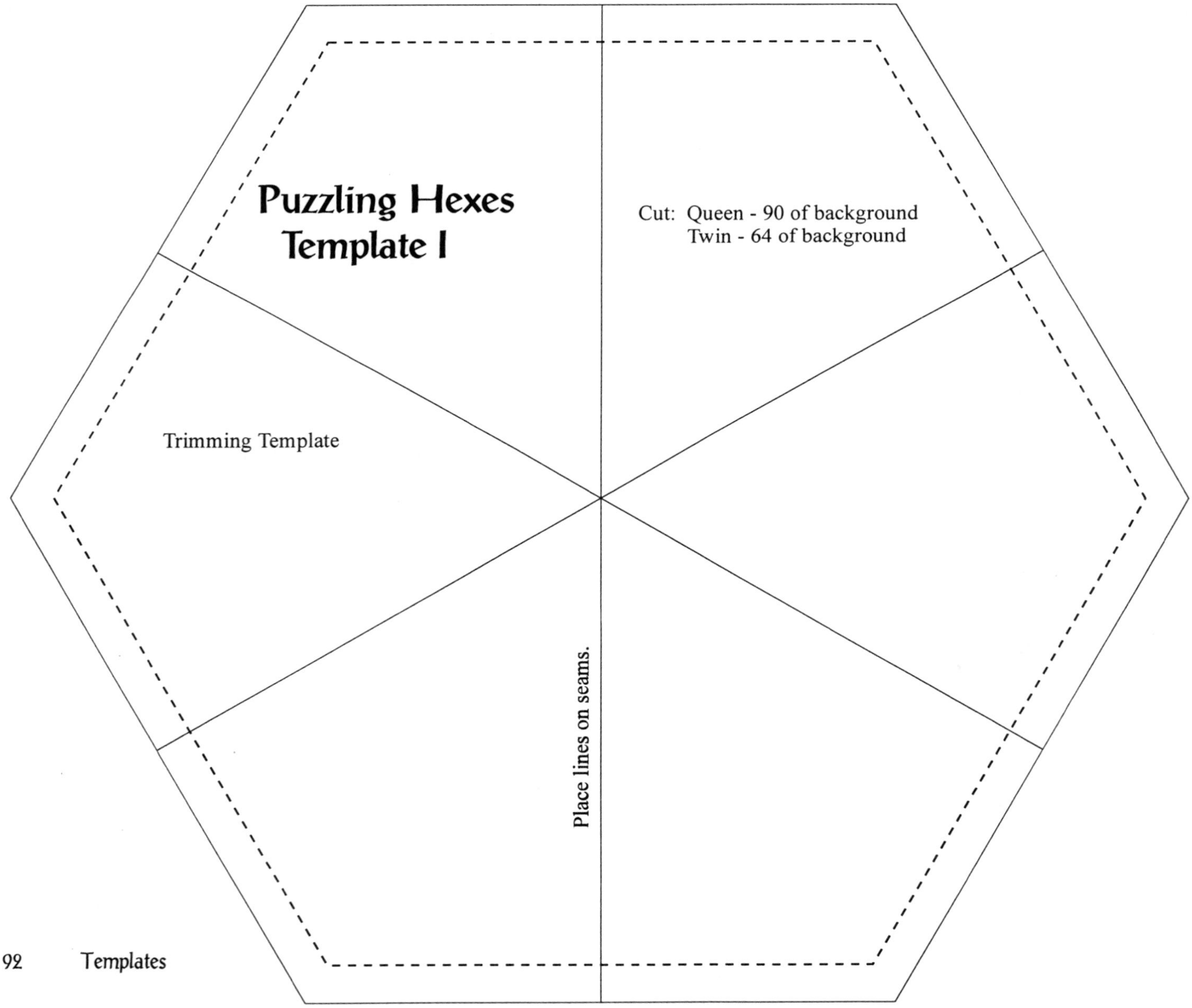

Puzzling Hexes
Template I

Cut: Queen - 90 of background
Twin - 64 of background

Trimming Template

Place lines on seams.

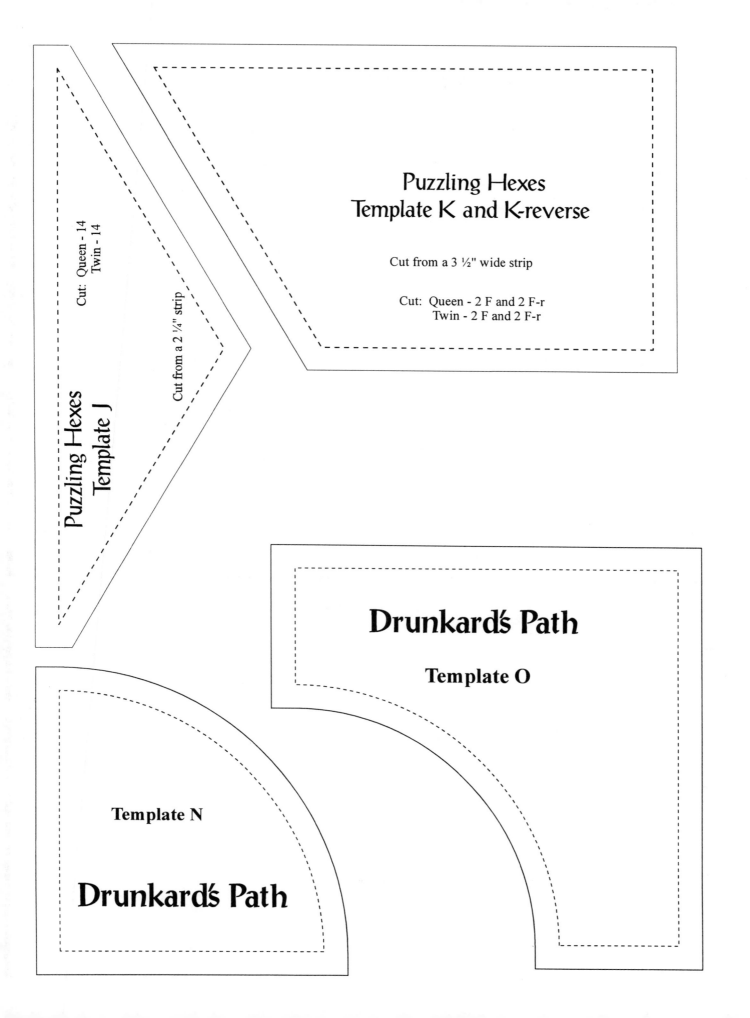

Puzzling Hexes
Template K and K-reverse

Cut from a 3 ½" wide strip

Cut: Queen - 2 F and 2 F-r
Twin - 2 F and 2 F-r

Puzzling Hexes
Template J

Cut: Queen - 14
Twin - 14

Cut from a 2 ¼" strip

Drunkard's Path

Template O

Template N

Drunkard's Path

Quilter's Cheat Sheet

Half Square Triangles

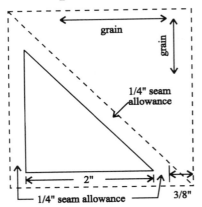

grain

grain

1/4" seam allowance

2"

1/4" seam allowance

3/8"

Finished Size + 7/8" = Cut Square

Quarter Square Triangles

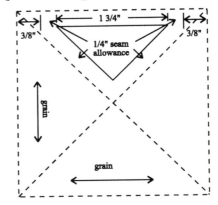

1 3/4"

3/8"

3/8"

1/4" seam allowance

grain

grain

Finished Size + 1 1/4" = Cut Square

Corner Triangles

A diagonal set quilt requires a half square triangle at each corner to complete the quilt top.

B

A

A = the known block measurement
B = the unknown measurement

A : 1.414 = **B**
B + 7/8" = Cut size of square
Each square will yield 2 triangles.

Setting Triangles

A diagonal set quilt requires quarter square triangles to fill in the gaps along the sides of the quilt top.

A

B

A = the known block measurement
B = the unknown measurement

A x 1.414 = **B**
B + 1 1/4" = Cut size of square
Cut square will yield four triangles.

Bias Binding

Bias binding is a must for quilts with curved edges, and a longer wearing treatment for bed quilts. Crossgrain binding has a single thread that runs the length of the outermost edge of the quilt. A worn spot can easily open up the length of the quilt. With a bias binding, the threads run across the edge diagonally. One weak thread can cause only local damage.
Yardage requirements are the same for crossgrain bindings and bias bindings.

Cut a single layer of yardage at a 45° angle. Stitch selvages together using a 1" wide seam. Trim selvages to 1/4" and press the seam open. Cut yardage into bias strips 2 1/2" wide. Stitch the strip ends together. Press the seams open. Fold bias strip in half, wrong side together. Bind the quilt in the usual fashion.

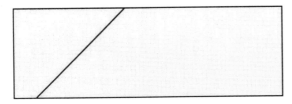

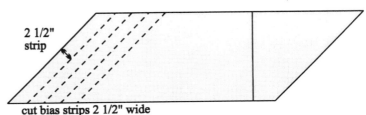

2 1/2" strip

cut bias strips 2 1/2" wide

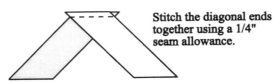

Stitch the diagonal ends together using a 1/4" seam allowance.

Standard Sizes

	Mattress	Batting	Quilt
Crib	23" x 46"	45" x 60"	37" x 52" - 56"
Twin	39" x 75"	72" x 90"	70" x 90" - 96"
Double	54" x 75"	81" x 96"	80" x 90" - 96"
Queen	60" x 80"	90" x 108"	90" x 96" - 100"
King	76" x 80"	120" x 120"	104" x 96" - 100"

Mattress size + desired drop = quilt size. *Drop* is the portion of the quilt that falls below the edge of the mattress. Consider the usage of the quilt when determining the drop.

Backing Yardages

Backing should be 6" to 8" larger than the completed quilt top. Yardage is figured on 43" of usable fabric width after shrinkage and selvage elimination. Measure the quilt top to determine the length and the width.

Single Length
Widths up to 37" = length + 6"

Two Lengths
Widths 38" to 80" = (length x 2) + 12"
Remove the selvages and sew one lengthwise seam. Press to one side.

Three Widths
Widths greater than 80" = (width x 3) + 18"
Remove the selvages and sew two crosswise seams. Press to one side.

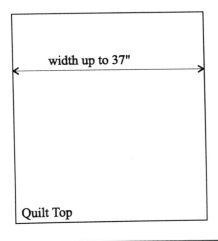

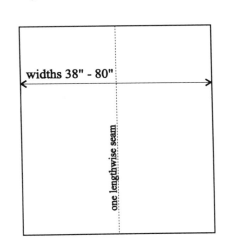

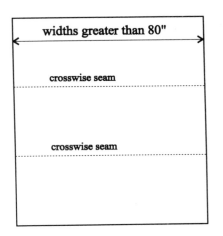

Mitered Binding

Stitch binding to the quilt edge. Start and stop the seam 1/4" from the quilt corner. Backtack at each end. Fold the strip away from the quilt top, and then down into position to stitch the second edge. Start and stop the seam 1/4" from the quilt corners. Continue in this manner around the quilt.

Draw lines **A**, **B**, and **C** as shown. Stitch on lines **B** and **C**. Trim excess and turn point right side out. Hand stitch fold in place.

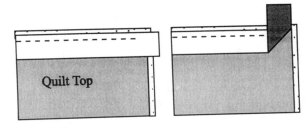

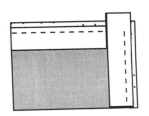

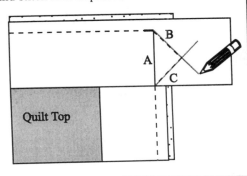

Meet the Author

Brenda Henning is a compulsive quiltmaker with a fondness for traditional design and a desire to incorporate today's speed-piecing techniques with yesterday's well-loved patterns. Brenda's machine sewing experience began at the early age of 10 on her grandmother's treadle sewing machine with the first quilt following at age 14. Brenda became a compulsive quilter in the mid-'80s, and began teaching quiltmaking in 1989, after her third child turned one.

Writing and self-publishing that work have been by-products of teaching quilting. Brenda is the author of: *Alaskan Silhouette Sampler, Sampler Schoolhouse, Scrap Quilts for Material Girls , and Stained Glass Flower Garden*, along with numerous individual patterns available under the label *Bear Paw Productions.*

Brenda lives in Anchorage, Alaska, with her husband, Richard, and their three children, Beth, Christi and Joshua. Two Rottweilers, Coco and Blue, (I'll bet you can't guess Brenda's favorite color!) share copious quantities of black dog hair with every quilt

that leaves the premises.

Brenda teaches regularly at The Quilt Tree and Quilt Works in Anchorage as well as for other shops and guilds throughout Alaska.

Sources

Specialty products used in the text are listed below. Please check with your local quilt shop for availability of the product before you contact the manufacturer directly. Support your local shop!

Omnigrid #96 Ruler
Omnigrid, Inc.
1560 Port Drive
Burlington, WA 98233

60° Clear-View Triangle Ruler
Clearview Triangle
8311 - 180th Street S.E.
Snohomish, WA 98296-4802
(360)668-4151

Roxanne's Glue-Baste-It
Roxanne International
85 Tuscany Way
Danville, CA 94506

Triangles on a Roll
Gridded Half Square Triangle Paper
Dutton Designs
P.O. Box 7646
Chandler, AZ 85246-7646